WICKED
NEWPORT

WICKED NEWPORT

KENTUCKY'S SIN CITY

Dr. Thomas Barker, Dr. Gary W. Potter
& Jenna Meglen

THE
History
PRESS

Published by The History Press
Charleston, SC 29403
www.historypress.net

All images are courtesy of the Kenton County Public Library.

First published 2008
Second printing 2009
Third printing 2009
Fourth printing 2013

ISBN 978-1-5402-1921-3

Library of Congress Cataloging-in-Publication Data

Potter, Gary W.
Wicked Newport : Kentucky's sin city / Gary Potter and Thomas Barker.
p. cm.
Includes bibliographical references.
ISBN 978-1-59629-549-0
1. Crime--Kentucky--Newport--History--20th century. 2. Corruption--Kentucky-
-Newport--History--20th century. 3. Organized crime--Kentucky--Newport--
History--20th century. 4. Criminal justice, Administration of--Newport--History-
-20th century. 5. Social problems--Newport--History--20th century. 6. Newport
(Ky.)--History--20th century. 7. Newport (Ky.)--Social conditions--20th century. 8.
Criminals--Kentucky--Newport--Biography. 9. Newport (Ky.)--Biography. I. Barker,
Thomas. II. Title.
HV6452.K4P68 2008
364.1'060976934--dc22
2008037357

CONTENTS

CONTENTS

INTRODUCTION

Newport, Kentucky, lies to the south of Cincinnati, across the Ohio River, and to the east of Covington, Kentucky, across the Licking River. It was incorporated in 1795 by James Taylor, the brother of Hubbard Taylor, who actually platted out the site, named it and took up residence on it in 1775. The city was named for the British explorer Admiral Christopher Newport, who captained the first ship from England to Jamestown, Virginia. Newport was a small river town, whose potential for importance as a major river port had been eclipsed by Cincinnati. By 1830, Newport still had only 715 inhabitants. Newport was a town thoroughly isolated from its neighbors. There was no bridge across the Licking River to Covington until 1854 and no bridge across the Ohio River to Cincinnati until the Civil War. Newport's economic identity would not become established until the late 1800s, when a large brewery and a large steel mill began operations in the town.

Newport would, no doubt, have been just another of the quaint, quiet, sleepy towns on the south shore of the Ohio River to the east of Louisville if it had not been for organized crime. Individuals and groups operating in the "hidden economy" of the United States would give Newport a distinctive identity for the entire twentieth century. Newport would become a legendary city in the history of American organized crime. In fact, Newport would share a designation as an "open-city" with only a handful of other towns, such as Hot Springs, Arkansas; Saratoga Springs, New York; Galveston, Texas; Hallendale, Florida; Phenix City, Alabama; and Biloxi, Mississippi. Open cities were communities in which politics, economics and crime became so enmeshed that separating one from the other was impossible.

They were cities where organized crime became the dominant influence, an influence that persisted for decades. Of all the nation's open cities, Newport had the longest run of unfettered criminal capitalism. In fact, Newport would become the earliest prototype of wide-open gambling later emulated in Las Vegas. Newport's importance as an organized crime entrepôt is what put the city on the map.

But why Newport, Kentucky? What was it about this town and this configuration of politics and economics that made it so attractive to criminal syndicates? Reporter Hank Messick attributes Newport's uniqueness to two factors. First, he claims that Newport was geographically isolated from the rest of Kentucky by bad roads and hilly terrain, requiring that it be both economically and politically autonomous. Second, he attributes Newport's uniqueness to cultural conflicts between German and Irish Catholic immigrants and anti-immigrant, Protestant, "Know-Nothing" elements in Kentucky. Messick argues that this rift in the local population doomed any common political purpose or initiative for most of the twentieth century.

There is much truth to Messick's observations. Certainly, Newport was isolated, even from its closest neighbors. The absence of bridges to Cincinnati and Covington for the first sixty years of Newport's existence clearly stunted its economic growth and allowed Cincinnati to develop as the primary river port in the area. Newport's distance from Lexington, Louisville and Frankfort, and the difficulty of travel, certainly separated it from the major centers of social, political and economic life in Kentucky, as well as making it difficult, and politically unrewarding, for governors to interfere in Newport's life, both legal and illegal.

Anti-immigrant bias was also well developed in Kentucky and in Cincinnati. In the 1840s, Newport's population swelled to six thousand people as a result of an influx of Irish and German immigrants. In the 1880s, a second wave of German immigration occurred. There is no denying that anti-immigrant feelings ran high in Kentucky in the mid-1800s. There was a large and active, although short-lived, Know-Nothing party preaching anti-immigrant politics, and there were acts of considerable violence, such as "Bloody Monday" in Louisville in which twenty-two people were killed on August 6, 1855, in anti-Catholic riots. Certainly, there were traditional divisions and deep-seated animosities between Catholics and Protestants in Newport. How debilitating these were over time to political reform is a matter of conjecture. Messick believes that these divisions prevented a united front against organized crime until George Ratterman's campaign for sheriff of Campbell County in the 1960s. Anti-German and anti-Irish prejudice did not enhance political cohesion.

INTRODUCTION

But there were other influences on the development of Newport, as well. Every river town on the Ohio and Mississippi had its share of vice and river piracy during the nineteenth century. While river piracy in Kentucky was most common west of Louisville on the Ohio, some occurred in the Northern Kentucky area. Similarly, while Natchez, Vicksburg and New Orleans would become the primary "vice districts" for nineteenth-century river commerce, Newport also had its small share of vice in the form of faro games and "hog pens" (floating river brothels).

But the primary influences on Newport's development as an open city can probably be identified in the economy and politics of the area. Despite the tendency to treat organized crime as an evil aberration in American history, the truth is far more complex. Organized crime, as demonstrated by every historical study on the subject ever conducted in the United States, is an organic, vital part of the communities in which it exists. Organized crime provides jobs, capital for reinvestment and a substantial injection of money into the local economy. It provides political contributions, under-the-table kickbacks, lucrative investment opportunities and election workers for political campaigns. It also provides an important social structure in communities that creates a buffer against the coarsest, most brazen criminal elements, who now are subject to social controls initiated by syndicates, and provides opportunities to make a living for a large number of very marginal people who might otherwise turn to more dangerous forms of predatory crime. Finally, and most importantly, organized crime exists only where there is demand for it. Organized crime does not create gamblers, drinkers, johns for the prostitution trade or illegal drugs and drug users. Organized crime simply establishes structures to meet that demand and profit from it. The relationship between organized crime and the communities in which it operates is highly symbiotic. The lesson of both historical and contemporary research on organized crime demonstrates universally that organized crime cannot exist where it is not wanted or tolerated. And in Newport, it was a welcomed guest.

Part One

SLOT MACHINES, HANDBOOKS AND LIQUOR

Pre-Prohibition Organized Crime

In the early twentieth century, prior to alcohol prohibition, Newport was the perfect place for outlaws, desperadoes, bank robbers and kidnappers to hide out from the law; so much so that it came to be known as "Little Mexico." The geographic and political isolation of Newport made it a good place to rest and relax in relative anonymity during those periods when the heat was on. It was also a place of opportunity for enterprising young criminal minds. In 1917, two such enterprising young men, Howard "the Hillbilly" Vice and Charles Kroger, introduced the first slot machine to Newport. Howard Vice came out of Clay County, Kentucky, and worked for a while as a bodyguard for Toledo, Ohio bootlegger Jackie Kennedy. When Kennedy was murdered by Pete Licavoli, who later became a major force in Ohio organized crime, Vice went to Newport to seek his fortune. There he linked up with Kroger, a Cincinnati native.

In 1917, the two men ordered a slot machine they had seen advertised in a magazine from the Herbert Mill's Company in Chicago. The slot machine was one of Mill's brand-new fruit-symbol gambling devices, a vast improvement over slow and unreliable earlier gambling machines. They placed the machine in a candy store, where it made about sixty dollars a week in profit, not an inconsiderable amount of money for one machine in 1917. Later, they moved the machine to a "beer garden," where it made even more money. But there was a problem. The machine kept breaking down, and parts had to be ordered from Chicago. It often took weeks for the spare parts to arrive, thereby cutting off the machines' income. Vice and Kroger grew tired of these interruptions and sold the machine to Lawrence McDonough and "Boots" Ortlieb. A few years later, Kroger was killed in an argument over bootlegging profits. Howard Vice went on to become something of a legend in early Newport organized crime lore.

McDonough and Ortlieb invested more capital in additional machines. They also solved the breakdown and repair problem by hiring a man to serve as a combination repairman/collector who would maintain a regular route to fix the machines and collect the coins. It was a highly successful endeavor. By March 24, 1917, the Campbell County grand jury was reporting:

> *The citizens of our county do not realize the magnitude of slot machine gambling. The daily income averages $8 per machine. It is estimated that about 150 machines are in operation. This means about half a million per year. The tremendous possibilities of corruption are plainly seen.*

The grand jury may have seen the "tremendous possibilities of corruption," but it clearly did not understand them. The judge overseeing the grand jury inquiry ordered Dayton Police Chief Frank Ortlieb ("Boots" Ortlieb's father) and Newport Police Chief Frank Bregal, whose son headed up a competing slot machine syndicate, to take charge of the cleanup. The slot machine syndicates seemed quite safe for the time being.

There were other forms of gambling in Newport at the time. Pool halls offered betting on either billiards or cards. With the advent of the telephone, bookmaking on horse racing became a fixture of many Newport taverns. However, prior to the 1920s, these gambling activities operated on the fringe of society and underground with little organization. That was to change with Howard Vice and Prohibition.

After selling his slot machine, Vice went back to hiring himself out as a bodyguard to bootleggers during Prohibition. But one evening, while playing in a craps game at the Gun Club, a local speakeasy, Vice went on one of those legendary runs of the dice and won $6,000 from the club's owner. The owner decided it was simply easier to give Vice the Gun Club than to pay the debt. So, Howard Vice, the hired muscle from Clay County, was now a speakeasy owner. Vice operated the Gun Club for several years, surviving several extortion attempts by early local crime syndicates. In fact, Vice was shot and wounded in one shakedown attempt. But it wasn't the threat of extortion that drove Howard Vice out of the illegal liquor business; it was actually the quality of the liquor itself.

Kentucky's Sin City

In the early days of Prohibition, sufficient quantities of bonded liquor had been diverted to the illegal market to supply demand. Vice relied on several local independent bootleggers who were running high-quality bonded booze into Newport. But as Prohibition continued, the supply of bonded liquor was depleted. Large organized crime syndicates in New York and Chicago had not, at this time, established the smuggling enterprises that would bring Canadian, European and Cuban liquor to the United States. Therefore, speakeasy operators relied more and more on home-brew. While there was an ample supply of home-brew in Newport, Vice didn't want to sell it. He decided that running liquor would be more profitable than selling it, so he sold the Gun Club and set up his own bootlegging enterprise. Vice bought a fleet of cars specially outfitted to carry large quantities of alcohol. He and his associates picked up liquor in seaport cities in Georgia and Florida and ran it to Cleveland and Detroit. At one point, he was invited to join George Remus's massive bootlegging operation in Cincinnati, but he declined and continued as an independent.

Howard Vice's career as a major organized crime figure came to an end as a result of a love affair. Back in Newport, Vice became entangled in an amorous triangle involving the owner of the Kentucky Inn, Charles Lafata, and a local woman, known only as "Miss Tiger Woman." The affair is characterized in local lore as a case of true love between Vice and Miss Tiger Woman, with Lafata playing the role of both cad and spoiler. But the dispute with Lafata also involved a question of whether Vice or Lafata actually owned the Kentucky Inn, a more substantive business-related issue. So, while the truth has probably been lost in the mists of time, it is probably more accurate, particularly considering the Kentucky Inn's reputation as a speakeasy and house of ill repute and the locally supplied moniker attached to the woman in question, to suggest a more complex business relationship. In any event, one evening Vice was drinking at the Kentucky Inn when Lafata confronted him. In the altercation that ensued, Lafata pulled a gun on Vice and Vice reciprocated. Who shot first is a mystery, but Vice's bullet wounded Lafata in the shoulder. At that point, another shot rang out—apparently not fired by Vice, but by some unknown person in the room—that killed Lafata. Howard Vice was arrested, charged with murder and convicted. With the aid of a duplicate key supplied by parties unknown, Vice simply unlocked the door of his Newport jail cell and left. Two years later, Vice was found in Nashville, Tennessee, and returned to Newport to serve his life sentence. Upon release from prison in the 1930s, Vice remained in Newport and, in partnership with local syndicate enforcer Albert "Red" Masterson, bought and operated a hog farm that supplied pork to the casinos. The hog farm also hid a 150-gallon still. Howard Vice would forever be enmeshed in some aspect of the liquor trade.

PROHIBITION AND ORGANIZED CRIME IN NEWPORT

In 1919, Congress passed the Volstead Act, which effectively outlawed the distribution, sale and consumption of alcohol in the United States by setting up an enforcement mechanism for Prohibition. Prohibition was a key event in the development of organized crime in the United States; it was no less important for organized crime in Newport.

First, as was the case almost everywhere else, Prohibition was a major impetus to the spreading of organized criminality. Otherwise legal businesses, like restaurants, taverns and cafés, now became "speakeasies," or in Kentucky parlance, "tiger blinds." This not only extended the scope of organized crime into otherwise legal activities, but it also increased geometrically the number of locations in a community where "vice" was practiced. Where illegality occurred with regard to liquor, it was a small step to also provide gambling, prostitution and the other vice-related goods and services. In addition, the sweeping nature of a Prohibition law, by definition, suddenly and dramatically increased the number of criminal actors in a community by automatically converting those whose activities were legal on one day into organized criminals the next day.

Second, the criminalization of drinking allowed the accumulation of massive sums of working capital for criminal enterprises. Prohibition was the biggest moneymaker for organized crime that the government ever invented. Prohibition demonstrated that making a widely demanded "vice" illegal and not vigorously enforcing the law inevitably turns the supply side of the supply-demand equation over to the crooks and gangsters. Later, gambling would fit in this equation. In testimony before the Kefauver Committee, Moe Dalitz, who became prominent in Newport gambling before moving on to respectability in Las Vegas, reflected on his days as a bootlegger:

> *Kefauver: As a matter of fact, you have been making a great deal of money in recent years, so I suppose from your profits from one investment you would then go ahead and make another investment. Now, to get your investment started off you did get yourself a pretty good little nest-egg out of rum running didn't you?*

Kentucky's Sin City

Dalitz: Well, I didn't inherit any money Senator...If you people wouldn't have drunk it, I wouldn't have bootlegged it.

During Prohibition, most people still drank. But now, illegality allowed for what political scientist Herbert Packer has termed a "crime tariff" to be added to the price. This artificially created organized crime tax ostensibly covered the additional costs of operating an illegal enterprise and compensated the participants for increased risk. What it accomplished in reality was an escalation in profit accumulation. From these profits, it was possible, as was the case in Newport, to fund new ventures in vice.

Third, Prohibition added a veneer of respectability to organized crime. The underworld, which previously had simply been a collection of pimps, madams, racketeers and gamblers operating in a segregated environment that ensured the delivery of services to customers, but which also ensured that "respectable" folk would have little or no contact with the vices if they so chose, now was invited into everyday life. Liquor for weddings, birthday parties, anniversary celebrations and the like came from the underworld. While it was unlikely that most middle-class families would invite a pimp into their parlor, a bootlegger was an entirely different matter.

Finally, Prohibition institutionalized corruption. Corruption was always present, but it was clandestine and discrete. Payoffs ensured that those who wished to participate in gambling, prostitution, opium smoking and the other vices could do so, but in discrete settings under established rules that shielded criminal enterprise from the public gaze. Prohibition changed all that. The public not only wanted vices tolerated, but it also wanted assurances that liquor would continue to flow. In many cities, and Newport was no exception, politicians began to appear publicly with bootleggers to allay public fear of liquor enforcement. Open bribery reassured drinkers that their nectars would continue flowing. Prohibition institutionalized public corruption as an appendage of American politics.

In Newport, these impacts were as real as anywhere else. Dozens of ostensibly legal establishments sold illegal liquor. In fact, according to Treasury Department estimates, there were over three thousand illegal speakeasies in the Cincinnati–Northern Kentucky area. Large-scale smuggling operations provided beer, wine, whiskey and gin to these businesses. Small-scale production operations became a common means of supplementing income. Oral tradition has it that there were so many backyard stills in Newport producing wine and brandy that the smoke from these stills blocked out the sun from 1919 to 1932. While this is no doubt a bit of nostalgic hyperbole, there is similarly no doubt that the production of "red" (illegal moonshine) liquor was commonplace in Northern Kentucky. It is well documented that in the early years of Prohibition many major syndicates, including those of Al Capone, Dutch Schultz and Meyer Lansky, purchased some of their stock in Newport, as well as in other Kentucky locales.

It is from these speakeasies that many later gambling locations were spawned. It is from liquor-based corruption that the payoffs that supported massive-scale gambling were organized. And it is from the early local liquor syndicates that most of the key actors in Newport organized crime emanated.

GEORGE REMUS, KING OF THE BOOTLEGGERS

George Remus had nothing to do with gambling and prostitution, but his impact on the organization of crime in Newport was enormous. Remus was a German immigrant who came to Chicago in 1876 at the age of three. He was by trade both a licensed pharmacist and a criminal lawyer, occupations that would position him well for Prohibition (1919–32). Even though he was a highly successful Chicago lawyer, he saw that his clients, although lacking in education and business acumen, were making more money much faster than he was. He reasoned that his abilities and his knowledge of the law, particularly the Volstead Act that enforced Prohibition, could work in his favor. Remus moved to Cincinnati, right across the river from Newport, at the beginning of the Prohibition era. At that time, 80 percent of America's bonded whiskey was made within three hundred miles of Cincinnati. There he built a bootlegging empire that, while short-lived, nonetheless had two major implications for Newport organized crime: 1) his bootlegging operation formalized corruption; and 2) his bootlegging syndicate would spawn many of the major actors in Newport gambling.

Remus's bootlegging enterprises were audacious and massive. As a pharmacist, Remus could buy bonded liquor from the Treasury Department for use in medicines, hair tonics and the like. He could then divert that liquor to illegal sales. Remus created several pharmaceutical companies and secured the federal permits necessary to buy alcohol. Federal Treasury agents estimated that Remus owned about 15 percent of the legal alcohol stock in the United States. It was with this legal liquor that Remus began his empire by diverting the legal liquor to the black market. But he didn't stop there. Remus parlayed the profits from his liquor diversion into the purchase of seven distilleries in Ohio, Indiana and Kentucky that had been closed

Kentucky's Sin City

by the Volstead Act. These distilleries had licenses to produce denatured alcohol for legitimate purposes, such as rubbing alcohol, varnish or cleaning materials. In Newport, the president of Wiedemann Brewery became one of Remus's major suppliers. The Wiedemann Brewery was, at one time, distilling one million gallons of alcohol for "industrial purposes." At least half of the alcohol was of the denatured variety used by Remus in making liquor. Remus put together a large distribution organization employing dozens of local criminals. Remus's bootlegging syndicate first moved its alcohol on the highways by the truckload, and then on the rails by the boxcar load, to local distribution sites. He was soon transporting liquor to all points within a five-hundred-mile radius. In one three-month period, Remus deposited over $2.7 million into local banks.

But Remus did more than organize the production and distribution of "white" (legally produced, rather than moonshine) liquor. He also organized political graft on a massive scale, recruiting contacts in police departments, courthouses and city halls in the tri-state (Kentucky, Indiana and Ohio) area. He was given the appellation of the "Gentleman Grafter." By his own accounts, he spent $20 million paying off police, judges and mayors to simply look the other way as his bootlegged liquor flowed into their jurisdictions. Remus is credited with teaching the art of graft to public officials in the area. While this may be overstated, especially in light of the fact that local politicians and law enforcement already were adept at taking bribes and "looking the other way," it is certainly true that Remus elevated the level of organization in local corruption to a point at which it became routinized. The regular, scheduled, weekly payoff became a way of life in Newport.

During Prohibition, however, local corruption was insufficient to maintain a criminal organization. It is in this regard that Remus differed from most of his more successful East Coast and Midwestern colleagues. While Meyer Lansky, Bugsy Siegel, "Dutch" Schultz, Al Capone and others had been able to neutralize, corrupt or otherwise protect themselves from Treasury Department agents, Remus ignored this area of vulnerability to his detriment. He perfected corruption at the local level, but he was unable to corrupt the Prohibition directors of Indiana and Kentucky, which caused his downfall. In 1922, Remus's operation was raided, and he and twelve of his associates were arrested, convicted and imprisoned. At the time of his arrest, George Remus's net worth was estimated at $70 million. Following his release from prison, his life took a bizarre twist (see text box). But it was the progeny of the Remus bootlegging operation who would use the web of corruption he created to establish post-Prohibition gambling as the major enterprise in the open city of Newport. Among the twelve who played a key role in Remus's bootlegging syndicate, and who would play a continuing role in organized crime in Newport, were Ernest "Buck" Brady, who ran transportation services for Remus; Peter Schmidt, one of Brady's drivers, who would open the Beverly Hills Club; Sam Schraeder, who would go to work for the Cleveland Four; and Albert "Red" Masterson, who would also work with the Cleveland Four as their local muscle.

CINCINNATI'S TRIAL OF THE CENTURY

In an ironic twist to the George Remus saga, his wife, Imogene, and a federal agent who had met his wife while Remus was in prison began carrying on an affair while he was in Atlanta Federal Prison. The agent left the Bureau of Prohibition and became Imogene's constant companion. Together, they bilked millions from Remus's estate—the estimates range from $2 million to $40 million. They also stole furniture and personal belongings from his mansion.

Three days after being released from prison—October 6, 1927—on the way to finalize their divorce, Remus chased his estranged wife into Cincinnati's Eden Park and shot her to death in front of their daughter and one hundred witnesses. The prosecutor at his trial was Charlie Taft, the twenty-nine-year-old son of the former president. At his trial, Remus represented himself and used the novel defense of not guilty by reason of insanity. At that time, this defense had not been used in an American courtroom. He ranted and raved during the trial, earning a contempt of court conviction, which was later overturned. His ranting and raving, coupled with the tale of infidelity by his wife and the man who had sent him to prison, won the sympathy of the jury, and it found him not guilty by reason of insanity. The state committed him to a mental hospital, but after a few months he was declared sane and released. The Remus trial became known as Cincinnati's "Trial of the Century."

During this same period, independent bootleggers also operated in the Newport and Covington area, some acting as suppliers to Remus and some on their own. These moonshiners were relatively safe from federal actions unless on the road transporting their wares. Federal judges, citing the Fifth

Amendment's protections of private property, were reluctant to issue search warrants unless direct evidence showed that a still was located on private property. However, many illegal stills were found when they overheated, exploded and caused fires. The worst of these disasters occurred in 1925, when a one-hundred-gallon still located in a chewing gum factory exploded. The resulting fire destroyed the plant, a house next door, three garages, three cars, a motorcycle and a horse. The damage was estimated at $25,000, a considerable sum at that time.

Conflict among the moonshiners was also extensive. The competition among warring independents led to beatings, gunfights and murders. Newport in 1926 had seven murders, a record for Northern Kentucky. The moonshiner wars left ten dead in just three months of 1927. No doubt the federal breakup of Remus's organization was a factor in the bloodshed. There is also no doubt that all the violence was not the result of battles between moonshiners; knife fights and shootings were also occurring in Newport's gambling halls and bordellos.

"DON'T COME OVER TO NEWPORT; IF YOU DO, YOU WILL GET IN TROUBLE."

These were the prophetic words of a defendant in a brutal murder case that took place on May 29, 1926, at number 317 Isabella Street. The Court of Appeals of Kentucky, in the March 28, 1928 case *Martin et al. v. Commonwealth*, described what took place at this address that Saturday night. The house at 317 Isabella Street was used as

a rendezvous for all sorts of law violators, both male and female, and in which many disreputable and prohibited acts and conduct were performed and engaged in. It was, in every sense of the term, a most disorderly house wherein intoxicating liquor was manufactured, sold and consumed by those who resorted there, including lewd women from Cincinnati and surrounding territory. Gambling was also indulged in…the establishment was a menace to peace and good order in that community.

PROHIBITION-ERA GAMBLING

The sale of illegal liquor wasn't the only organized crime enterprise flourishing in Newport during Prohibition. By the mid-1920s, gambling began overtaking bootlegging as Newport's main vice and "tourist" attraction. A vigorous reform campaign in Cincinnati after World War I had forced many of the gamblers and their operations over the Ohio River and into Newport. Their customers followed them, expanding Newport's position as Cincinnati's playground. The Queen City was enhancing Newport's sobriquet as "Sin City." The large-scale political graft and police corruption put in place by Remus added to Newport's problems. An article in the *Kentucky Post* on March 3, 1926, sums it up:

> *Reports from many sources in Newport indicate a laxity of law enforcement, such as never existed before. Not only are Newport gamblers running full blast; but many Cincinnati gamblers, said to be chased from the Queen City, are also located within the confines of Newport. Every branch of the law enforcement body has succumbed to the reign of gambling. The police are inactive, the commonwealth attorney and his detectives and the sheriff's office apparently unmindful of what is going on.*

Newport's Safety Commissioner Chris Elbert didn't appear to be overly concerned when he stated, "It is a well-known fact that that gambling has existed in Newport. It has existed for years and will continue to go on as usual after we are gone."

Gambling syndicates were also in place, as we have seen with regard to slot machines, which by now were even located in grocery stores. But other gambling operations, mostly supplying bookmaking services related to horse racing through local handbook operations, were also well established. The extent of handbook gambling is difficult to estimate for the 1920s and early 1930s. But two attempts at enforcing the state gambling laws give us a fairly good indication that it was widespread and profitable.

ENTER THE TROOPS—
COLONEL DENHARDT AND THE STATE GUARD

The precursor to the first attempt to enforce the state gambling laws began with labor strife and the use of the state guard. On Christmas Day 1921, the state guard (later to be the National Guard) was sent into Newport under the command of Colonel Henry H. Denhardt to break strikes at the Andrews Steel Mill and the Newport Rolling Mill. Denhardt came well prepared to deal with the Steelworkers Union. He brought several hundred soldiers, including a machine-gun unit and a tank unit. Denhardt's task was to deploy this massive show of force to protect nonunion strikebreakers working at both plants. The steelworkers were not intimidated, and for several days following the arrival of troops, a running gun battle was underway in the streets of Newport between strikers and their supporters and Denhardt's state guard. Eventually, the gunfire stopped, but the tension between strikers and troops continued. The troops withdrew from Newport. The use of troops against strikers was certainly not unheard of in this period of American history, but what happened next gave this troop deployment a distinctly Newport-style twist.

Early in 1922, while the strike continued, the newly elected Newport City Commissioner W. Case Thomasson announced his intentions to lead a campaign against gambling and other forms of vice in the city. Support for cleanup campaigns was a persistent theme in Newport and would continue to be for the rest of the twentieth century. Sometimes the calls for reform came from religious groups with strong moral qualms about gambling, drinking and prostitution. Sometimes local businessmen would join in hoping to improve the business climate in the downtown area. And often, in Newport as in almost every other American city, politicians would initiate the call for reform, not so much for reform's sake, but rather for the benefit of whatever syndicate interests they represented as opposed to the interests of the syndicates they were trying to clean up.

The response to calls for reform were quite predictable in Newport. The police made a few perfunctory arrests; the courts allowed still fewer perfunctory convictions and then levied some small fines. A few slot machines were confiscated, a still or two smashed and the cleanup campaign ended with a claim of total success. The bootleggers, pimps, madams and gamblers tightened up their business practices and lay low for a few weeks, then business resumed as normal.

Whether Commissioner Thomasson was a sincere reformer or merely a politician maneuvering for the benefit of his organized crime supporters is impossible to discern. Nonetheless, on January 4, 1922, Commissioner Thomasson ordered Newport Police Chief Frank Bregel to act against gambling and other forms of vice. Thomasson was quite direct in telling Chief Frank Bregel that, "unless commercialized gambling and vice are run out of Newport, I will put somebody in your place who will get results."

Thomasson's cleanup campaign met with some support and some approval. Local ministers convened a meeting of the faithful at the Temple Theater at Sixth and Monmouth Streets in Newport to show support. The *Kentucky Post* editorialized that the cleanup effort was a good beginning, but it could only succeed if the people of Newport rallied behind it.

Then the reform effort took a bizarre turn. Shooting and violence again erupted between the steelworkers and management, and the governor ordered Colonel Denhart back to Newport. Denhardt threw the force of his troops behind the reformers. Because Denhardt was acting on authority from Frankfort, he was beyond the control of corrupt local officials. He was also beyond the control of local politicians, who may have been able to advance the cleanup campaign without the additional divisiveness caused by Denhardt's authoritarian actions.

Denhardt acted quickly, apparently with the support of Commissioner Thomasson. He reasoned that, since the handbook operators were dependent on telephone services, both to receive bets and to get the results of horse races, the first target of his campaign would be the telephone company. Denhardt sent troops to the Citizens Telephone Company with a demand that the company supply him with a list of all unlisted telephone numbers in Newport. Since handbook operators did not have listed numbers, Denhardt reasoned that all of them would be identified somewhere on the list of unlisted numbers. Similarly, Denhardt dispatched troops to the local newspaper stand with an order that the owner provide him with a list of all regular customers who purchased the *Daily Racing Form*. Once again, he assumed that such a list would contain the names of most regular local illegal bettors. The newspaper dealer and the telephone company resisted Denhardt's orders. But later it was learned that, acting "unofficially," a telephone company employee had turned over the list of eighty-five unlisted numbers to Denhardt, thereby enabling him to identify the local of several handbooks in Newport.

Meanwhile, the local police were making their perfunctory gambling arrests. A few bookmakers, mostly those unaffiliated with any larger syndicate operations, were arrested, assessed small fines and sent back to work.

By the end of January, Newport Mayor Joseph Hermann had decided that a little reform was too much reform. Announcing that he had "good reasons," the mayor began pardoning arrested gamblers.

One of the more important raids and arrests in this cleanup campaign occurred on January 25, 1922, when a raid of the York Café, at 411 York Street, led to nineteen arrests on gambling charges. It seems as though a sizeable handbook operation was operating out of the second floor of the establishment. Campbell County Sheriff Louis Tieman was also raiding vice locations outside of Newport. About the same time as the York Café raid, Tieman moved against Edward Steinkamp's roadhouse on Alexandria Pike in Clifton.

The federal government even got into the act by swearing in two local religious leaders, Elmer Correll and James Wood, as federal Prohibition agents assigned to North Kentucky. Concomitant with this development was a raid by Colonel Denhardt's troops on several illegal stills in Newport, which resulted in the arrest of six men on liquor charges. In a letter to Governor E.P. Morrow, Denhardt justified using state troops in the liquor raids by stating that a general atmosphere of lawlessness pervaded Newport.

On February 16, in a brazen display of brute force, sixty-eight of Colonel Denhardt's troops surrounded the Campbell County Courthouse in Newport. The building was sealed, and arrest warrants were served on Mayor Herrman, Police Chief Bregel, Campbell County State Attorney Conrad Matz, Campbell County Police Officers John Sheehan and Charles Bullet and Campbell County Detective Edward Hamilton. All were charged with failing to discharge their official duties in that they knew about illegal activities and refused to act against them. Under state law, they were all subject to terms of up to two years in jail and $2,000 fines.

The next day, on February 17, Denhardt called out his tanks in an ostentatious display in which he had the tanks roll over and crush confiscated slot machines and stills in the street outside the courthouse.

The first signs of dissent outside of Newport's city hall began to appear on February 19, 1922, when the *Kentucky Post*, in an editorial, suggested that the denial of basic political and legal rights was not a solution to the problem of vice and gambling. The *Post* said that crime and corruption emanated from years of neglect in Newport, but the use of troops was a dangerous excess.

On February 19, Denhardt's troops and the newly appointed federal Prohibition agents, no doubt moved by the Spirit, as well as the presence of spirits, raided thirty Newport speakeasies and eleven stills. Thirty-eight people were arrested, firearms were seized, slot machines were confiscated and vehicles loaded with illegal alcohol were towed away. On that day, state troops searched every car leaving Newport.

The raids were not without incident. The word of what was happening spread quickly through Newport, and angry crowds of citizens, no doubt including some still highly perturbed strikers, began to gather. The crowds shouted insults at the troops and a few rocks were thrown. Colonel Denhardt had to call out more troops to disperse the angry protestors.

In response to the protests and to the *Kentucky Post* editorial, two additional Newport city commissioners, J.B. Morlidge and Charles McCrea, dispatched a letter to Governor Morrow indicating their support for Thomasson and Denhardt.

Despite a large number of indictments by the grand jury in February 1922, about seventy-five in all, the fervor for reform was beginning to fade. In April 1922, the Campbell County grand jury refused to indict any of the elected officials and police arrested by Denhardt, with the exception of Police Chief Bregel, who was indicted for conspiring to possess and distribute illegal liquor. Nonetheless, the chief continued to serve, and there is no public record of his "trial" on the indictment to be found. However, the chief was later charged with influencing voters in the elections of November 6, 1923, and the primary of October 20, 1923. Commissioner Thomasson further charged him with inefficiency and neglect in the performance of duty in 1922, 1923 and 1924. In a hearing before the board of commissioners, he was found guilty and demoted to patrolman. Chief Bregel appealed to the Campbell Circuit Court, which upheld the findings of the board of commissioners. He then appealed to the Court of Appeals of Kentucky. The Court of Appeals reversed and remanded the case for further proceedings. There is no evidence that any further action was taken against Chief Bregel, and he remained chief of police until 1932.

Whatever local support for Colonel Denhardt remained after the raids of February, it was quickly dissipated by two more authoritarian decrees. First, the good colonel decided to enforce Kentucky's "Blue Laws," which in essence forbade any business activities on Sundays. Second, he issued a decree banning the playing of baseball in the occupied "Mill Zone" he created around the steel plants, which encompassed much of Newport. Banning business and baseball was simply too much for Newport.

Before the situation could deteriorate further, the strike was settled, and by the end of April, state troops withdrew from Newport. With Denhardt's troops gone, local police became less vigilant about gambling, drinking and other forms of vice. The raids virtually stopped. The grand jury suddenly decided not to indict any longer, juries suddenly decided not to convict any longer and Campbell County judges suddenly determined that all the evidence seized by Denhardt's troops was inadmissable because of the lack of proper search warrants.

Colonel Denhardt tried to parlay his Newport strikebreaking and cleanup campaign into a political career. In 1923, he was elected lieutenant governor of Kentucky on the Democratic ticket. In 1927, he was defeated in an effort to get the Democratic nomination for governor. Four years later, on election day 1931, he was shot in the back by a political rival. Denhardt survived the shooting and went on to be named state adjutant general. In 1936, Denhardt was the defendant in a celebrated murder case. It seems that his girlfriend was shot and killed near LaGrange. Denhardt was arrested and charged, but the jury could not reach a verdict. A second trial was scheduled, but on the evening preceding that retrial, Denhardt was shot to death. His deceased girlfriend's three brothers were accused of the Denhardt murder, but they were quickly found not guilty by a jury, which felt they killed the colonel in self-defense.

As the 1922 reform campaign demonstrates, there was more than a little gambling, illegal liquor distribution and generalized vice in Newport. It further demonstrates that illegality was not universally condemned by the citizenry, nor by elected and police officials. In 1927, the *Kentucky Post*, in another series of articles under the headline "Somebody is Giving the Court the Ha-Ha," published after the Campbell County grand jury returned no gambling indictments, named the locations and provided sketches of handbooks. The local politicians were just not interested. Local controversies notwithstanding, it would be another nine years before another outsider attempted to clean up Newport.

THE CAMMACK RAIDS

On June 19, 1931, Newport was subject to another effort at reform from the outside. Kentucky's attorney general, J.W. Cammack, arrived in Newport and personally took control of the city and county police. Cammack then staged three raids on gambling "dens." These "dens" were primarily bookmaking operations where people would gather to bet on horse races from around the country and wait for the results to come in through organized crime's wire service. The first raid was at 339 Central Avenue, where a handbook operated by Bob Cottingham was closed down. Cottingham and five of his employees, Cal Wittstein, John Flynn, Thomas W. Curry, Walter Schott and M.H. Oliver, were arrested, and approximately 150 gamblers were ordered to leave. The second raid, at 524 Monmouth Street, was not as successful. Harry Blackman, alleged to be associated with a Detroit gambling syndicate, apparently operated a handbook on the second floor of the Monmouth Street address.

This early connection to Detroit-based organized crime is interesting because three later arrivals would both have Detroit connections. The

Levinson brothers, Ed, Mike and "Sleepout" Louis, got their start in the Detroit underworld, as did Moe Dalitz, one of the leaders of the Cleveland Four. Both the Cleveland Four and the Levinson brothers would play pivotal roles in Newport's glitzy casino-gambling era. Blackman had apparently been tipped off that the raiders were coming. According to press accounts, about one hundred gamblers left the Monmouth Street handbook. Blackman was not there to be arrested, but he turned himself in the next day. The third raid was on a handbook operated by Louis Biehl on the corner of York and Front Streets. Biehl operated a café in front and a handbook in the back. Biehl also apparently had advance knowledge of the raids as well, and according to witnesses, he sent his customers to the six other gambling establishments operating on that block.

Newspaper accounts of the raid make it clear that none of the establishments felt it necessary to remove their gambling paraphernalia, and all three were connected to the national wire service as a means of getting racing results from around the country. Additionally, it is clear that other handbooks did not feel the need to close, and they were, in fact, operating with the gambling action clearly visible from the street. It is fair to say that Attorney General Cammack's criticism of local police, judges and city officials for not enforcing the law seems justified in view of the fact that gamblers did not fear the destruction of their equipment and that other gamblers not specifically named in the Cammack raid warrants felt no reason to close down. Second, the presence of wire service connections indicates that local bookies were tied to larger national syndicates, particularly Chicago, where, most likely, the wire service being used in Newport was located.

Part Two

ORGANIZING CRIME
IN THE 1930S

One of the major problems for organized crime coming out of Prohibition was figuring out what to do now that liquor was legal again. Some Prohibition-era criminals went straight and established much of the modern distilling and brewing industry. Others realized that they had the money and expertise to mange another illegal monopoly: gambling. Prohibition showed them that when there was a demand for illicit goods and services, gangsters were the only ones who could supply it. Some, like Owney "the Killer" Madden, Meyer Lansky and Bugsy Siegel, made the transition to large-scale illegal casino gambling in New York, Arkansas, Florida and, later, California and Las Vegas. For some organized criminals, the transition was deadly. Dutch Schultz, the "Beer Baron of the Bronx," lost his life in a steakhouse in Newark, New Jersey, after attempting a bloody incursion into the New York numbers racket. Lucky Luciano made a disastrous foray into the prostitution business in New York. Faced with an open revolt by madams and bookers (individuals who supplied women for the brothels), Luciano ended up in Dannemora Prison, sentenced to thirty to fifty years.

For others, as the history of Newport reveals, the end of Prohibition created an opportunity. In 1933, with the repeal of Prohibition, the bootleg gangsters came out of the Great Experiment rich and powerful, with an illegal monopoly over liquor, and sensed that another monopoly existed for them. That illegal monopoly was the control of gambling. Speakeasies had provided multiple forms of gambling. After Prohibition, gambling was another vice that enjoyed widespread appeal for the American public. The laws prohibiting gambling reduced the gangsters' competition, giving them a legally imposed monopoly. They would soon move their money and muscle into bookmaking (sports and race), policy (the poor man's lottery), gambling machines and illegal casinos.

From a purely rational approach to crime, crime occurs when inclination and opportunity come together under a low-risk situation. This was certainly the case in Newport, Kentucky. The Newport gangsters had the inclination honed in the pursuit of illegal activities during Prohibition, the opportunities were numerous in Newport and the low-risk situation existed in Newport's history of political and police tolerance, corruption if you will, and tolerance by the citizens and business community.

BUST-OUT JOINTS

In Newport, the transition from Prohibition was no less perilous for some. The liquor business was still a lucrative pursuit, despite the re-legalization of alcohol. As late as 1935, federal agents raided a house at 114 West Second Street and arrested seven people, including a pharmacist. The men were engaged in the illegal distilling of high-quality whiskey. A fifty-gallon barrel of their product and expensive distilling equipment were seized in the raid. But despite the persistence of the liquor trade, small-scale gambling became the backbone of the local underground economy. A number of small casinos, known as "bust-out joints," gambling venues where the games offered had such a high house advantage that customers left the establishment "busted-out" or broke, operated in the downtown area. It was not uncommon for winners, or those who still had money remaining, to be given knockout drops in their drinks and then robbed. Customer relations were dedicated to taking as much money as possible from the patrons. Most of these clubs also had horse parlors and sports-betting operations on the premises. In fact, for most of the clubs, these handbooks were still their major sources of revenue.

On Central Avenue in Newport, the 316 and 345 Clubs (named for their addresses) were operating. The 316 Club was operated by alumnus of the Remus bootlegging syndicate, Taylor Farley. The 345 Club was run by Emile Bridwell. The Bridwell brothers, Emile, James, Ralph and Ray, would run several bust-out joints over the years, but their primary illicit business was prostitution. These Jackson County, Kentucky natives ran a series of brothels over the next three decades in Newport, a remarkable record of longevity. The Club 314 operated at 314 West Fourth Street and was another of the small bust-out joints in town. In the late 1930s, a gambler named Arthur

Dennert opened the 633/Flamingo Club at 633 York Street. This club later became one of Newport's most popular casinos under the direction of the Levinson brothers.

Outside of Newport in the 1930s, a couple of casinos also operated, including the Avenue in Bellevue, a town a little northeast of Newport, and the Beacon Inn, located a little south of Newport on Licking Pike. Also, right outside of Newport was the Green Lantern nightclub, run by Ernest "Buck" Brady, George Remus's transport director. The Green Lantern, located at 311 Licking Pike, opened in August 1930. The incorporators of the Green Lantern were three Newport attorneys, Daniel Davies (who had unsuccessfully defended Howard Vice in his murder trial), Jack Luboff and Charles Teakin. In thoroughly segregated Newport, the Green Lantern was primarily a gambling casino for African Americans. The Green Lantern appears to have been a relatively successful and well-run operation. Being

CARPET JOINTS

From 1933 through the 1950s, organized crime operated gambling openly in much of the United States. These carpet joints were modeled after the opulent Saratoga Springs, New York casinos. Hidden ownership and corruption of public officials were essential to the illegal casinos. Liquor and restaurant licenses were always put in the name of a local businessman, who was also responsible for making payoffs. The casinos were usually located in rural areas, with the local police and politicians as silent partners. Gambling, liquor, restaurants and big-name entertainment were provided.

The carpet joints run by Meyer Lansky and his partners in Hallendale, Florida—ten miles from Miami Beach—became known as a "little Las Vegas before its time." Paul Whitman, Sophie Tucker, Harry Richman and Joe E. Lewis appeared in these Florida carpet joints. The Chicago Outfit, the Cleveland Four and New York émigrés like Owney "the killer" Madden ran carpet joints in Hot Springs, Arkansas; Cincinnati and Cleveland, Ohio; Covington and Newport, Kentucky; Omaha, Nebraska; Houston, Texas; Biloxi, Mississippi; Council Bluff, Iowa; and New Orleans, Louisiana. The partners in the illegal casinos, such as Moe Sedway, the Levinson brothers, Moe Dalitz and Benny Binion, would resurface with Meyer Lansky in Las Vegas in the 1950s.

outside Newport, it was beyond the reach of local police. The club also had a no-weapons rule vigorously enforced by "Buck" Brady, which required that all patrons be frisked for weapons before entering.

The handbooks and emerging casino business in downtown Newport and its surrounding environs set the tone for the future development of criminal enterprises and also created the conditions for future conflicts over those criminal enterprises. But Newport would have remained little more than a vice district for Cincinnati, with small-time prostitution and gambling run by local entrepreneurs, had it not been for two developments. The first was the establishment of two high-class casinos, called "carpet joints" because of the presence of carpeting as opposed to the more familiar sawdust on the floor, in the area (see text box). And the second was the interest displayed in those carpet joints by a major criminal syndicate of national importance.

PETER SCHMIDT AND THE BEVERLY HILLS CLUB

One of the associates of George Remus who would have a major impact on the organizing of crime in Newport was Peter Schmidt. Schmidt had been one of Remus's truck drivers and was one of the twelve men arrested with Remus. Upon his release from prison, Schmidt used the money he made in bootlegging to buy a hotel on Monmouth Street in Newport, which he renamed the Glenn Hotel, after his son. The hotel had a notorious history. It had served as a hideout for fugitives during Prohibition. Among its two most famous clients were Bob Zwick, a hijacker and hired gun, and Dave Jerus, one of Al Capone's gunmen who participated in the St. Valentine's Day Massacre.

Initially, Schmidt offered illegal alcohol for sale, a few slot machines to amuse his patrons and a very small casino and handbook. In order to supplement his income from the hotel, Schmidt also operated a thousand-gallon-a-day still on Kentucky Drive right outside Newport. The Kentucky Drive still was one of the targets of treasury agents who raided and destroyed it. During the raid, Schmidt shot a federal officer, an act that earned him another five-year stint in prison.

Back in Newport, after serving his prison sentence, Schmidt expanded the casino at the Glenn Hotel, but it was still a small-scale operation. He envisioned a much larger, much more elegant gambling venue, complete with good food and entertainment, much like Lansky's casinos in Saratoga, New York, and Broward County, Florida, or like the Cleveland Four's Arrowhead

Club. Using profits from the Glenn Hotel, Schmidt purchased a former speakeasy named the Old Kaintuck Inn three miles south of Newport in the town of Southgate. He totally refurbished the old club, renamed it the Beverly Hills Club and opened it as Newport's premier carpet joint. The Beverly Hills Club was the first real casino in the Newport area.

THE CLEVELAND FOUR

Just as Pete Schmidt was getting the Beverly Hills Club up and running, the Northern Kentucky/Cincinnati area fell under the gaze of a syndicate of national importance with far-flung illicit business interests. That syndicate went by many names—the Mayfield Road Mob, the Cleveland Syndicate, the Silent Syndicate and the Cleveland Four. Of those appellations, the Cleveland Four most closely captures the essence of this organization. Named for the four leaders of the syndicate, Moe Dalitz, Morris Kleinman, Louis Rothkopf and Sam Tucker, the Cleveland Four had a long history and wide-ranging interests. These bootleggers first came together to monopolize rumrunning across Lake Erie. They soon moved into other profitable and illegal enterprises for four decades. Their success was predicated on two basic business principles: 1) there were enough illegal revenues for everyone to share and 2) some management responsibilities should be left to local operators. These two principles would lead to successful operations in Newport and elsewhere. Their philosophy of "enough for all" fit in very well with another gangster cabal, Meyer Lansky and his associates. Arguably, along with Lansky and his associates, the Cleveland Four was one of the most powerful syndicates in the United States and a defining influence in the organization of crime throughout the twentieth century.

Each of the governing members of the Cleveland Four brought his own unique experiences to the organization, assumed primary responsibility for specific enterprises of the organization and left his own clear mark on organized crime. Moe Dalitz was a native of Detroit, where he was an early member of the Purple Gang, a syndicate involved in the "protection racket," strikebreaking and bootlegging. He was a friend and mentor of the young Jimmy Hoffa, who would rise to prominence as president of the Teamsters Union. Dalitz left Detroit for Cleveland and rumrunning across Lake Erie in 1925. Morris Kleinman was a Cleveland native who started out running a brewery in Cleveland and ended up supervising bootlegging for the Cleveland Four through Canada. Louis Rothkopf, also a Cleveland native, had expertise in the construction and management of stills. He took a major role as a supervisor of the syndicate's many alcohol production facilities both domestically and internationally. Finally, Sam Tucker was an immigrant from Lithuania who supervised the purchase, maintenance and operation of the fleet of boats used by the syndicate during Prohibition.

Closely allied with Meyer Lansky and Bugsy Siegel in New York, the Cleveland Four were bootlegging liquor from Canada and operating a nationwide distribution system. By 1930, they were partners with Lansky in several large distilling operations in both Cuba and Ohio, and partners with the Bronfman's in what would later become Seagram's. In the early 1930s, the Cleveland Four, just like Lansky, began establishing illegal gambling casinos in the Cleveland area as a probable post-Prohibition enterprise. By the 1950s, the Cleveland Four were joining Lansky and his friends in the Las Vegas expansion at the world-famous Sands and Desert Inn Hotels.

Although the Cleveland Four distributed liquor in the Newport area, their first direct move into metropolitan Cincinnati came with the assassination of Dutch Schultz. The Dutchman owned a racetrack outside of Cincinnati named the Coney Island Racetrack. Within days of Schultz's demise, the Cleveland Four took that track over, renaming it River Downs, a track that continues to run today. Shortly thereafter, they acquired ownership of Latonia Park, a dog track in Florence, Kentucky, right outside Newport, which was later converted to a thoroughbred track and, still later, renamed Turfway Park. Although they only operated Latonia as a dog track for thirteen days before it was closed down by the state police, their ownership of the track helped them establish a presence in Northern Kentucky. They were also busy duplicating the success of their "carpet joints" in Cleveland, with a new casino on the banks of the Ohio River, outside of Cincinnati, called the Arrowhead Club.

The Arrowhead Club was the Cleveland Four's first move into the Cincinnati area. It was used as the stepping stone into Northern Kentucky. The club was located in the Branch Hill suburb of Cincinnati. It opened in the 1930s and was financed by the syndicate and operated by locals, Joe Bauer and Harold and Sam Nason. As usual, the gambling operation was made possible through the local "fix." However, the unique nature of the fix arrangement caused its downfall. No one in the county would talk to Bauer about a fix, but, according to Trimble, he located a local Baptist minister who would act as a bagman. The minister stipulated that the gamblers would never know where and to whom the money went. This arrangement worked well until August 1937, when Joe Bauer suddenly died. The Nasons did not know the identity of the bagman, and he never came forward. The

Nasons continued to operate the club even after being told by the county prosecutor to close. Finally, the county prosecutor raided the Arrowhead Club on November 19, 1937, and closed it down. The syndicate was already making plans to move into Northern Kentucky, where the fix arrangements were well known to all parties involved.

SYNDICATING THE BEVERLY HILLS CLUB

The Beverly Hills Club was an unqualified success, with frequent visits by celebrities such as Jimmy Durante and Frank Sinatra. However, that success caused problems for Schmidt. One of the early visitors to Schmidt's casino was Moe Dalitz. Dalitz clearly liked what he saw and thought the Beverly Hills Club would be a fine acquisition for the Cleveland Four. Dalitz offered to buy it or to take Schmidt in as a partner. The Cleveland Four had established a pattern of acquiring gambling properties but keeping the local operator as a "frontman." Such an arrangement was usually quite lucrative for the frontman, getting the cash up front for the sale of the property and "points," or a percentage of the profits from the casino on the back end. But Pete Schmidt wasn't interested in selling or acquiring new partners, no matter how enticing the offer. The Cleveland Four, on the other hand, were not used to being refused. Schmidt's casino was subjected to minor acts of vandalism and a practice called "ding-donging," which primarily consisted of individuals coming in and urinating in the lobby. The harassment was principally the work of Schmidt's old compatriots in the Remus gang, Albert "Red" Masterson and Dave Whitfield, assisted by Larry McDonough, who headed up one of the local slot machine syndicates. In 1936, there was a fire at the Beverly Hills Club. The casino was destroyed, and the five-year-old niece of the caretaker, Carl Fillhardt, was killed.

David Whitfield, Sidney Diehm and Edward Garrison were indicted for the crime of willful murder, committed by setting a house on fire and burning an infant to death. They were charged as principles and for aiding and abetting the crime. At trial, the caretaker testified that he was awakened by the sounds of breaking glass as three men broke in downstairs to set the fire. He positively identified Diehm and Garrison as being in the house before the explosion and fire. Whitfield bought three five-gallon cans, but not the gas, the night before and told the storekeeper that he needed them to "get gasoline to carry out to the country." Diehm pleaded guilty and was sentenced to life in prison. Court testimony reveals that Garrison told the sheriff after his arrest that it was the first time that he had ever burned a child or killed a baby. He told the sheriff he could not sleep. He was found guilty and sentenced to life in prison.

The evidence against Whitfield was circumstantial. On the night of the fire, all three men had been drinking at Whitfield's bar. On the same night, Whitfield bought the three five-gallon cans. Witnesses saw three men running from the fire. Whitfield also hid Garrison, who was badly burned setting the fire, in the attic of a friend's house for several days. He also brought a doctor to the attic three times to see Garrison. It was at the friend's house where the sheriff arrested Garrison, and he made his incriminating confession about killing a baby. Whitfield was found guilty and sentenced to life in prison. He appealed his conviction, and after several years in prison, the Court of Appeals of Kentucky reversed his conviction and remanded the case for a new trail. The court stated that, although there was credible evidence (ill will toward Schmidt, he was seen in the company of the two men who confessed to the fire, three men were seen leaving the fire scene, he hid Garrison) to suggest that he had engaged in a conspiracy with Diehm and Garrison, there was little evidence that he had aided and abetted the crime. He was not retried.

The conspiracy theory and a set of strange events might well point to another conspirator. On the night of the fire, another of George Remus's old compatriots, Albert "Red" Masterson, purchased several canisters of gasoline. When he was asked what the gasoline was for, Masterson said that everyone would be able to read about it in the next day's newspaper. "Red" Masterson was a man with a reputation in Newport, and that reputation revolved around violence. He had been arrested during Prohibition, on December 23, 1925, for robbing a handbook in Elmwood, Ohio. After serving a brief prison sentence, he was arrested again on April 29, 1931, as the result of a shootout at the Duck Inn on Licking Pike, in which a man named Elmer McCabe, another local resident with a bad reputation for violence, was killed. Masterson claimed self-defense, and the local judge agreed.

Just a year prior to the Beverly Hills Fire, on February 28, 1935, Masterson had been arrested again, this time in connection with the murder of John Rosen. Rosen was a former fighter and was closely connected to the Chicago "Outfit," Al Capone's old syndicate. Rosen and another man were sitting and talking in a parked taxi at the corner of Sixth and Monmouth Streets in Newport. Masterson was walking past when Rosen called to him and waved him over to the cab. What they talked about is, of course, not known, although some speculation from the Newport police centered on Masterson's role in providing protection to local gambling operations from incursions by nonlocal syndicates. This certainly could be the case. Masterson had a local nickname of "the Enforcer" because he hired out as muscle when he was needed by local gamblers. On the other hand, there is considerable evidence that, by this time, Masterson was in the employ of the Cleveland Four, who, while they were definitely moving into North Kentucky, were still an out-of-town syndicate. Nonetheless, according to reports at the time, as Masterson approached the cab, he pulled out two .38-caliber, snub-nosed revolvers and fired eight shots, six of which hit Rosen, killing him instantly. Police officers nearby quickly arrested Masterson, who was still standing there with the guns in his hands. Masterson once again pleaded self-defense in the Rosen killing, and once again the judge agreed, setting him free.

The purchase of a couple gallons of gasoline was not the only thing that connected Masterson to the Beverly Hills Club fire. Edward Garrison, who had previously been active in the New York gangs of Legs Diamond and Dutch Schultz, was an acquaintance of Masterson. Whitfield was also a friend of Masterson's and yet another alumnus of the George Remus bootlegging operation. After Whitfield was released from prison and returned to Newport, he was rewarded by being given the properties that originally were operated by Howard Vice.

Whether the Beverly Hills Club fire was an action initiated by the Cleveland Four or something related to a more local dispute will never be known with certainty. The possible role of Red Masterson in the fire certainly enhances suspicion that the fire was an act initiated by one or another crime syndicate. Reporter Hank Messick was certain that the fire was directly connected to Moe Dalitz and the Cleveland Four. The presence of Edward Garrison lends some additional credence to Messick's suspicions because it doesn't seem likely that local Newport-based gamblers would have access to a New York organized crime figure. But, in retrospect, it seems a very clumsy way for an organization with immense financial resources and pervasive political connections to handle a problem. A plausible, although certainly not proven possibility, is that the fire was a clumsy attempt by local organized criminals, Masterson in particular, to ingratiate themselves with the Cleveland Four. Certainly, Masterson and whomever he was acting on behalf of may have ruffled some feathers in Chicago with the Rosen killing. In 1936, it is a fair statement that the three most successful criminal syndicates in the United States were the Chicago Outfit, the Cleveland Four and the Lansky-Siegel "Eastern" syndicate in New York. The protection provided by affiliation with the Cleveland Four would have been substantial.

Furthermore, it is highly likely that Edward Garrison was not in Newport at the behest of local organized criminals, but was fleeing the turmoil in New York related to the Dutch Schultz killing. In fact, Garrison was not present at the Palace Chop House when the Dutchman and his gang were killed only because he missed the train from New York. Considering Schultz and those around him had engaged in such wanton violence that Meyer Lansky, Bugsy Siegel and Owney Madden felt compelled to respond in kind, a decision by Garrison to take some rest and relaxation in Newport would have been quite rational. So a variety of unhappy circumstances may have led to a poor decision at the local level in Newport, a pattern that would be repeated consistently when local hoods were left to their own devices.

Peter Schmidt, however, was not deterred by the fire and rebuilt the Beverly Hills Club. It reopened in April 1937 as the Beverly Hills Country Club, in a gala affair attended by locals, some celebrities and politicians and governors from four states. Crystal chandeliers, oak paneling, plush blue carpets and gilded gold leaf–pattern wallpaper made the new Beverly Hills an even more elegant gambling venue. Although there were other opulent casinos operating in the United States at the time, the glitz and glamour of the reopened Beverly Hills Club defined the model that would become common in Las Vegas when the mob moved there. But the phoenix risen from the ashes was an even greater target for the Cleveland Four.

In the summer of 1937, a group of men armed with submachine guns robbed the Beverly Hills Country Club. Vandalism and "ding-donging" intensified. Schmidt responded by hiring heavily armed guards, but acts of harassment continued. Schmidt even approached an organized crime group from Toledo as possible partners, probably to provide him with some additional protection. For some three months, he actually leased the Beverly Hills Country Club to this Toledo group. But they had no interest in a run-in with Dalitz, Kleinman, Rothkopf and Tucker and quickly pulled out of the deal. Schmidt finally gave up. He sold the club to the Cleveland Four for a small down payment and additional future payments from club profits, a deal considerably inferior to the one he had been originally offered. In 1940, Charles Lester, a local attorney and a dominant, if not the main, figure in Newport's sordid saga for over three decades, handled the legal sale of the Beverly Hills Country Club from Peter Schmidt to Sam Tucker. The official sale occurred on November 18, 1940. Lester's growing role in the sordid history of Newport's reign as Sin City became clear in a civil suit arising from the earlier Beverly Hills Club fire (see text box). The Cleveland Four now had their "carpet joint" in Newport. Peter Schmidt retired to his Glenn Hotel, at least for the time being.

FILLHARDT V. SCHMIDT ET AL.

In a bizarre twist to the fire at the Beverly Hills Club, Carl Fillhardt, the caretaker, sued Pete Schmidt, alleging that Schmidt had never informed him of the threats, warning and notices of being burned out. Fillhardt alleged that this negligence led to his injuries and the death of the child. At first, Fillhardt approached a lawyer named Daniel W. Davis to represent him. Davis could not do so at the time because he was connected to the Whitfield prosecution. Davis suggested that another lawyer file the case and handle it until such time as he would be free to take over. A strange set of circumstances, a common occurrence in Newport's history, led to them finding Charles Lester. When Davis and Fillhardt approached the courthouse looking for the other lawyer, they found the city and the courthouse in general chaos because of the Great Flood of 1937. Charles Lester was the only lawyer in the courthouse. Because the statute of limitations would soon bar any civil action, they chose Lester to file the case. It ended up being a bad decision.

Lester, without approval of Fillhardt and Davis, settled the case for $2,500. Fillhardt refused to sign the settlement check, and the bank would not cash it without his signature. Undaunted by this, Lester got a cashier's check from Schmidt, cashed it, kept the money and somehow convinced someone in the county clerk's office to mark the case as settled. Fillhardt, sometime later, checking on the status of his case, discovered the fraud. He then sued Lester. In 1942, the Court of Appeals of Kentucky, citing judgment obtained by fraud, reversed the judgment.

JIMMY BRINK AND THE LOOKOUT HOUSE

The Beverly Hills Club wasn't the only "carpet joint" in Northern Kentucky. Over in Covington, across the Licking River in neighboring Kenton County, Jimmy Brink had opened the Lookout House. Jimmy Brink was a Cincinnati native who had been involved in local, small-time bootlegging. In 1933, Brink opened the Lookout House in a large frame house that stood above Covington and had been a central point on the underground railroad before

Emancipation. The Lookout House, located on a hill off the Dixie Highway, was a huge building that contained several cocktail lounges, a restaurant-showroom and, of course, a casino with large picture windows that allowed patrons to look out at the Cincinnati skyline, and presumably allowed local law enforcement to look in, had they been so inclined.

In April 1938, state authorities indicted Brink on forty-five counts of illegal gambling. The court issued an injunction against gambling at the Lookout House, but local authorities declined to enforce it. Two witnesses who had been instrumental in indicting Brink were beaten and subsequently declined to testify. The Lookout House was back in business, which was both good and bad news for Jimmy Brink.

Having acquired the Beverly Hills Country Club, the Cleveland Four were now taking notice of Brink's operation at the Lookout. A desire to expand their successful Kentucky holdings was part of the allure of the casino in Covington. But a more important tactical reason spurred Cleveland Four envy. The Lookout House was in Kenton County. The Beverly Hills Country Club was in Campbell County. Grand juries, which were required for any investigations or indictments, operated on staggered schedules. In other words, when the grand jury was in session in Campbell County, it was not in session in Kenton County. That meant that, with two "carpet joints" in neighboring counties, the Cleveland Four could close the one in the county with a grand jury in session. While corruption virtually guaranteed a smooth operation of gambling, acquisition of the Lookout House would guard against unwelcome judicial inclinations toward reform, or a grand jury that turned out to be hostile.

Once again, it was Sam Tucker who entered into discussions with Brink. Tucker was now living in Covington and managing the Northern Kentucky operation of the syndicate. Brink was well aware of the problems the Cleveland Four could cause and of the potential benefits of collaboration with a powerful, national syndicate. The syndicate offer was generous. Brink got $125,000 up front, a great deal of money for the 1930s; he got to keep 10 percent of the Lookout House; he was given 10 percent of the Beverly Hills operation; and he could stay on as manager. It was Cleveland Four policy to keep locals in day-to-day charge of their operations, and Brink benefited by becoming their frontman at the Lookout House.

The Cleveland Four were also looking to increase profits and efficiency at the Lookout House. To this end, they brought in two of the best gambling "mechanics" available, Alvin Giesey and Sam "Gameboy" Miller. Giesey was brought in to act as the accountant for the Lookout House, a vital task for any casino, but all the more vital for an illegal casino trying to conceal much of its revenue. "Gameboy" Miller took over the operation of the casino itself, managing the games and supervising dealers and table action.

The acquisition of the Beverly Hills Club and then the Lookout House changed the nature of organized crime substantially in Northern Kentucky. Prior to this time, gambling had been primarily a local institution, run by local entrepreneurs. The casinos had been small, rough, coarse places of business, mixing prostitution with gambling, designed to fleece players of their money as quickly and efficiently as possible. In fact, handbooks had played a much more important role in gambling, with bookmaking being a bigger volume business and being far more profitable than casinos. The carpet joints changed all that. Now, well-financed, honest games were offered to major players. The carpet joints effectively removed all the high rollers from locally managed "sawdust joints."

The carpet joints offered more than gambling. They had good restaurants and entertainment. The biggest names from New York and Hollywood were playing their showrooms. The carpet joints brought Newport into the casino era. They also attracted out-of-town action. In the 1940s and early 1950s, when air travel was not common and Las Vegas existed only in Bugsy Siegel's imagination, Newport was no more than an eight-hour train ride for over 60 percent of the U.S. population. The carpet joints gave players a reason to get on those trains. Finally, the carpet joints changed Newport in one other profound way. They established a major national syndicate as a power on the local scene. No local organized crime figure had the resources or power to take on the Cleveland Four. Soon the Cleveland Four would be joined by other out-of-town syndicate operators, and the open city of Newport would bloom into a 1940s gambling Mecca.

The Levinsons, the Bermans and Meyer Lansky

The 1930s in Newport ended with the arrival of the Levinson brothers, Ed, "Sleepout" Louis and Mike. The Levinsons grew up in Chicago, but they made their mark in organized crime in Detroit, where they ran a couple of casinos and played an active role in the newspaper-circulation wars of the 1920s. Their entrance into Newport was of major importance because the Levinsons directly represented the interests of another major, national syndicate headed by Meyer Lansky. While Lansky and his partners often worked in close collaboration with the Cleveland Four, their presence in Newport both provided a mitigating influence, now that two powerful syndicates were represented, and in some ways a greater threat to local syndicates and operators. It was clear by the end of the 1930s that those who "got along" with the powerful outside syndicates would profit handsomely, and those who did not would operate only at their sufferance.

The Levinson brothers simply forced Art Dennert out at the 633/Flamingo Club. The Flamingo was in downtown Newport at 633 York Street, but unlike the other downtown clubs, it was upscale and was about to go further upscale. The 633/Flamingo was a very large club with a bar and cafeteria in the front and the casino in back. The Levinsons also operated a major bookmaking parlor at the back of the casino. With a huge neon sign in front, the Flamingo was hard to miss.

On the other side and in the next block was the Yorkshire, at 518 York Street. The Yorkshire was run by Joe and Martin Berman (a.k.a. "Miller" in Newport), two gamblers who were Lansky's employees and/or partners in a number of earlier New York ventures. The Bermans had gained control of the Yorkshire in 1944 from Jimmy Brink. The Yorkshire was a three-story brick building with a seventy-five-hundred-square-foot casino on the first floor and a race and sport book in the back. The expensive carpets left no doubt that this, too, was an upscale joint.

The Cleveland Four also moved into the downtown area. They took over the Yorkshire Club, which was both a casino and a bookmaking operation. While the casino was profitable, the real money was in the handbook. The Cleveland Four were paying social security taxes of $200,000 a month at the Yorkshire and would, in later years, report to the Kefauver Committee that their monthly action at the Yorkshire was about $2 million in bets. The Cleveland Four had also taken over the Merchants Club on Fourth Street, which was being managed for them by Albert "Red" Masterson, perhaps as a reward for his earlier fidelity. By the early 1940s, Cleveland Four interests in Newport and the surrounding environs became so intense that Sam Tucker relocated to the area from Cleveland to oversee consolidation and expansion. The influx of syndicate money from Cleveland and New York fueled a massive expansion in Newport gambling in the early 1940s. Benefiting from those investments were not only syndicate-associated organized criminals, but local independents, as well. Casino gambling had arrived as a major commercial enterprise.

OTHER CASINOS OF THE 1940s

Many local operators also opened casinos in downtown Newport in the 1940s. These operations were smaller, less classy operations than the syndicate casinos. But it wasn't their size that caused concern in Cleveland and New York. First, the sheer prevalence of gambling was becoming a problem. It wasn't competition that the national syndicates feared, because they appealed to a very different type of gambler, but the fact that the sheer number of casinos was hard, even for corrupt local officials, to ignore. But a greater source of concern was the fact that these smaller "bust-out" joints ran rigged games. Cleveland and New York interests understood for years that it wasn't necessary to rig gambling. The sheer grind of mathematics meant the house would win, and would win big. But for smaller, and sometimes greedier operators, the grind was not enough. They introduced some games, like Razzle-Dazzle, that, while honest, had such an immense house advantage. Razzle-Dazzle was a game imported from Cuba that made use of six dice in a metal cage that was spun. In order to stay in the game, players had to keep doubling their bets. The big win was coming on the next spin of the cage. The big win never came. They also rigged roulette, a game favored by less cerebral players because of its lack of any useful strategy, and craps, a game at which large sums of money could be won or lost on any single roll of two dice. In order to guard against a run by players, some casinos kept loaded dice at the ready. Once again, complaints emanating from rigged games were not in the interests of syndicate operators.

The smaller casinos were opening everywhere. At 613 Monmouth Street, "Big Jim" Harris opened the Stork Club. Harris is best remembered for his ownership of the infamous Hi-De-Ho Club in neighboring Wilder. Several casinos opened that catered primarily to the African American population of Cincinnati in what was still a very segregated America. The Copa, at 339 Central Avenue; the Alibi, at 310 Central Avenue; the Rocket, at the corner of Second and York Streets; the Sportsman's, at 228 West Southgate Alley; the Varga; and the 222 Club (which would later be relocated next door to Covington) were all primarily black establishments.

Outside of Newport, the Club Alexandria had opened at 2124 Monmouth Street, about halfway to Beverly Hills Country Club in Southgate. The Alexandria Club could accommodate only about three hundred players. The Grandview Gardens, at 15 Wildrig Street in Wilder, was primarily a restaurant, but it had a small casino in the back. What had been the Beacon Inn on Licking Pike in Wilder became the Primrose Club in the 1940s, when it was acquired by Buck Brady. Brady was yet another of the alumni of

Remus's bootlegging operation. He invested his Prohibition-era profits in purchasing and remodeling the older casino. Brady believed that the rural setting of the Primrose Club would keep him safe from either of the national syndicates operating in Newport at the time.

There were also a few casinos opening up in Covington. The Kentucky Club opened at 627 Scott Street, and the Rocket Club (not affiliated with the Rocket Club that would open later in Newport) was at 417 Scott Street. The Dogpatch was a very small casino on the river in Covington, and another small casino called the Teddy Bear Lounge operated outside of Covington on the river. The Club Kenton was located near the corner of Main and Kenton Streets. The Covington casinos, with the exception of the Lookout House and the Kentucky Club, were much smaller than their Newport neighbors.

PROSTITUTION IN NEWPORT

Newport's prostitution industry also benefited greatly from the rapacious growth of gambling in the 1930s and early 1940s. Prostitution was certainly not a new enterprise to Newport in the post-Prohibition era. As early as the Civil War, troops garrisoned in Cincinnati would cross the Ohio River into Newport to make use of Newport's numerous brothels. But it wasn't until the 1930s that prostitution became highly organized and routinized in Newport and the surrounding cities.

Prostitution took many forms, some of which still survive today, but one unique aspect of prostitution in Newport was the influence of the city's system of one-way streets. Many residents of Northern Kentucky worked across the river in Cincinnati. When residents were going to work, they crossed the Ohio via Monmouth Street, a one-way thoroughfare leading into Cincinnati. When they returned, they used York Street, a one-way thoroughfare leading back through Newport. Some, but by no means all, prostitution was organized to accommodate this traffic flow. Brothels on or adjoining Monmouth Street were called "day houses" because they were open during the morning and afternoon to accommodate travelers to Cincinnati. The luncheon trade from the city across the river could get a "quickie" before returning to work. Brothels on or adjoining York Street were called "Night Houses" because they opened in the late afternoon and ran into the early evening, accommodating travelers back to Northern Kentucky and visitors from Cincinnati. This system was Newport's version of the early fast-food industry, providing quick "drive-up" services to customers. By the 1940s, there were three hundred women working in the brothels of downtown Newport, an area less than one-square mile in size. At one time in the 1940s and 1950s, there were nine brothels within two blocks of the police station. As late as 1959, the Fourth Street Grill was located across the street from the police station.

Of course, not all prostitution was centered on traffic flow. Some of the larger, more pricey brothels opened in the late afternoon and stayed open all night for the convenience of casino patrons. Newport was a pioneer in yet another type of prostitution: bar girls. Bar girls were dancers, waitresses or entertainers working in the many strip clubs (now euphemistically called "gentlemen's clubs") operating along Monmouth Street. In return for purchasing drinks, or more likely expensive "champagne," customers would receive the attentions of bar girls. Bar girls were paid a percentage of the house's take on the drinks they sold. The larger one's liquor bill, the greater the attention offered; the higher the level of enthusiasm exhibited, the more physical the contact provided. While bar girls are primarily a strip club phenomenon, some of the lower stakes, "bust-out" casinos, offered similar services.

Newport brothels had an ongoing arrangement with Cincinnati taxi drivers, who would funnel business in their direction. Any out-of-town traveler or visiting businessman who inquired about prostitution services would be taken to one of the Newport brothels. In return, the cabbie received a 40 percent kickback from the fees realized by the brothel. Competition between prostitution outlets was intense, and the cabdrivers were an important means for "advertising" their wares. Considering that about one million out-of-town visitors came to Newport each year before World War II, the referrals from taxi drivers were an important source of revenue.

Outside of Newport, in Wilder, one of the most famous brothels in America was in operation, the Hi-De-Ho Club. The Hi-De-Ho was primarily a brothel, although it did have a small casino operation as well. It was owned by James "Big Jim" Harris, the marshal of Wilder. Patrons of the Hi-De-Ho could drink at the bar and gamble at the casino on the first two floors. If they desired more physical pursuits, they could proceed to the top two floors.

Marshal Harris successfully operated the Hi-De-Ho until 1951, when state police raided the establishment. Under Kentucky law, in incorporated cities like Newport the state police had no jurisdiction unless they were invited in by local police. But Wilder was an unincorporated municipality, and the state police needed no invitation to act there. The raid was provoked by two factors. The Hi-De-Ho was taking gambling business away from the Cleveland Four's Latin Quarter, a casino they would acquire later in the 1940s, and they were busily lobbying their supporters in Frankfort for relief. In addition, the Hi-De-Ho's brothel operation was also engaged in blackmail. Harris had wired the rooms and gave his sex workers "scripts" from which they would try to elicit clients' names, addresses, wife's names and children's names. Sometime, after the client returned home, Harris would call and explain how embarrassing it might be for the audio tape to surface, suggesting that $5,000 would ensure the destruction of the tape.

"Big Jim" Harris was indicted by a grand jury in 1955 on prostitution charges. To a large degree, his indictment was the result of Cleveland Syndicate complaints about his blackmail operation and the continued growth of the Hi-De-Ho Club as a gambling venue. Harris also made the mistake of trying to shake down Cleveland Four operatives for $10,000. Now they would use the grand jury to close him down. Witnesses from the 1951 raid testified against Harris. Harris was represented by Charles Lester, who seemed to not take the trial very seriously—he simply didn't show up. Harris was sentenced to three years in prison and was now officially out of business.

By the early 1940s, gambling and prostitution were thoroughly institutionalized in Newport. The out-of-town casino owners brought in new money and new players. They were consolidating their dominant positions in gambling, while at the same, perhaps unintentionally, fueling an expansion of locally owned and operated vice. While the Cleveland Four and the Eastern Syndicate of Meyer Lansky and Bugsy Siegel had clearly been good for the Newport underworld, tensions were beginning to develop between the locals and the syndicates. And while the remainder of the 1940s would see a further consolidation of syndicate gambling, it would also see new and emerging conflicts between syndicate and local interests that would be played out in a number of bizarre ways.

1. Flamingo Club.

2. Exterior of the Beverly Hills Country Club.

3. Inside the Beverly Hills Country Club.

4. Inside the Lookout House.

5. Meyer Lansky's mug shot (circa 1920s).

6. Club Alexandria.

7. Vivian Schultz's brothel.

8. Inside the Latin Quarter.

9. Merchants Club.

Above: 10. Bar at the Latin Quarter.

Left: 11. Screw Andrews.

Right: 12. George Ratterman with two campaign workers.

Below: 13. The Sportmans Club.

14. La Madames Cocktail Lounge.

15. The Monmouth Street strip.

16. Video poker gambling machine raid, West Side Café, 1981.

17. Talk of the Town.

Part Three

SYNDICATE TOWN AND NEWPORT-STYLE REFORM

By the beginning of the 1940s, both prostitution and illegal gambling were widespread, well established and legally protected in Newport. These illicit businesses represented criminal entrepreneurship by both local residents and syndicates of national importance. This local-versus-national nexus is an important distinction in the development of organized crime in Newport, creating both opportunities and tensions that would play out for the remainder the 1940s. To recap, first, the character of illicit operations differed markedly between local enterprises and those affiliated with larger syndicates. Gambling operations run by locals tended to be "sawdust" joints and "bust-out" joints. "Sawdust" joints were small, crudely furnished, inhospitable gambling venues. "Bust-out" joints were casinos with many games designed to simply fleece the player, such as the dice game Razzle-Dazzle. If the players couldn't be fleeced at the tables, bust-out joints featured the attentions of bar girls, women who danced and were paid by the drink for enticing customers to treat them. Joints featuring bar girls also uniformly featured prostitution, but at a much higher total price (drinks plus the fee for a prostitute) than the brothels. The brothels themselves were also exclusively operated by local entrepreneurs.

Syndicate "carpet joints" were a different proposition. They offered honest games, albeit with a substantial built-in house edge. They were well appointed, comfortable and professionally run. Prostitution, while available to soothe the nerves of high rollers, operated on what would be known as the "Dalitz" system once it was relocated to Las Vegas's Desert Inn and was not a major profit-making venture of the house. Under the Dalitz system, the only prostitutes allowed to work the casino were employees of the casino, waitresses, dealers, showgirls and hat-check girls. If a female employee wished to engage in prostitution, she had to be approved by management, and her name was listed with the pit bosses who would make the referral.

Syndicate-affiliated casino managers saw the local bust-out joints as a problem for three reasons. First, they fleeced the players, meaning overall gambling revenues would be diluted. Second, they attracted unwanted attention because of complaints over their games, the openness of prostitution and the crudeness of their management. Calls for reform and law enforcement intervention invariably centered on bust-out joint activities. Finally, the local operators made it difficult to organize a collective approach to corruption or collective strategies in calming the occasional public protests, particularly from the churches, over gambling. The profit-intensive nature of the bust-out joints made them resistant to temporary closings, concessions to reformers or toning down the less-attractive aspects of their operations. In addition to all of these concerns, the way the syndicate had muscled some local operators out of business, such as the Cleveland Four takeover of the Beverly Hills from Pete Schmidt, also caused lingering resentment and tension. Those resentments, tensions and no small amount of greed began to manifest themselves in 1943, just about the time that Newport had settled down for a long run as an open town.

CHARLES LESTER, PETE SCHMIDT AND THE CLEVELAND FOUR

Charles Lester had been under retainer as an attorney to the Cleveland Four. Whether it was avarice, opportunity or simple bad judgment that motivated Lester is unclear, but in 1943 he switched sides in the Newport underworld. Lester began to conspire with Pete Schmidt, who still had hope that he would become Newport's premier illegal gambling boss, despite the presence of two powerful national syndicates.

In September 1943, Lester and Schmidt made their move. The local judge, who was on the Cleveland Syndicate's payroll, was out of town, meaning that any legal actions would have to be heard by the visiting jurist. Lester filed a civil suit naming ninety-two people as operatives of the Cleveland Syndicate and demanding that an injunction be issued requiring the local police and prosecutors to enforce Kentucky's gambling laws. A similar move in 1930 against houses of prostitution had led to a motion for disbarment against Lester. The disbarment proceeding was later overturned. In the 1943 suit, Lester recruited Jesse Lewis, an entirely unconnected and apparently honest deputy attorney general, as co-complainant. Lester and Lewis went to a courthouse in a neighboring county and found a judge willing to sign a restraining order against illegal casinos and ordering the Newport police to raid them and confiscate illegal gambling equipment. Lester returned to Newport with the injunction, assembled police raiding parties before all the

---

LESTER'S 1930 DISBARMENT PROCEEDING

During the summer of 1930, Lester appeared before Campbell County Circuit Judge Caldwell twice to seek injunctions against brothels in Newport. The second time, the judge told Lester to "quit bothering me about these damn whorehouse cases." Lester received $250 compromise fees for each case. All the cases were settled. Later, in charging the Campbell County grand jury, Judge Caldwell made the following statement:

> *It is a matter which I desire you to thoroughly investigate pertaining to the circumstances and real motives in the filing of a number of injunction suits in an alleged cleanup drive against women operators of alleged disorderly houses in Newport.*
>
> *Rumors are current that graft and protection money have been paid in connection with these injunction suits and the operators have had money extorted from them. It is also rumored that attorneys have been involved in these graft charges. This is a serious matter and nothing should be left undone in making a thorough probe. If the evidence warrants, indictments should be returned against all concerned in any unlawful practices.*

Nine charges were brought against Lester. He was acquitted of two charges and found guilty of seven in a trial presided over by Judge Caldwell. Lester's attorneys asked that Judge Caldwell vacate the bench because of the bad blood between the two, citing as evidence the charge to the grand jury. The judge refused. The Court of Appeals of Kentucky overturned the conviction because of the judge's refusal to recluse himself.

---

casinos could be warned and led raids on the Beverly Hills, the Merchants Club, the Yorkshire and apparently, for sake of appearances, Pete Schmidt's Glenn Rendezvous. Schmidt took only a marginal hit because, obviously, he knew in advance what was happening and hid much of his equipment. The syndicate-connected casinos did not fare as well, having over $100,000 worth of gaming equipment seized by the police. Five people were arrested and indicted on gambling charges.

The raids had been a bold ploy by Lester. But Newport, being Newport, was quick to offer a debilitating countermove. Campbell County officials ordered the seized equipment returned within days. The five indicted men never faced trial and were, in fact, all elected to public office in the next election as a clear repudiation of reform. But the Lester-Schmidt alliance would create problems in Newport for the next two decades, and Lester would play a major, although unintended, role in the eventual downfall of illegal gambling in the city.

By 1948, Lester and Schmidt were ready to try another strange gambit. They recruited a wandering street minstrel named Robert Siddell to run for mayor. They rationalized that controlling the mayor's office would give them some leverage against the Cleveland Four. But Siddell lost, and a syndicate-backed candidate won and promptly ordered a raid on Schmidt's Glenn Rendezvous Club. With some reason, Schmidt was concerned about further retaliation. So, in order to keep the Glenn Rendezvous out of the hands of the Cleveland Four, he sold it to the Levinson brothers and Arthur Dennert, thus placing it squarely under the control of allies of Meyer Lansky.

Whether it was just happenstance or whether the Cleveland Four were genuinely miffed at the sale of the Glenn Rendezvous will never be known. Nonetheless, Art Dennert was killed in an automobile accident. Oral tradition in Newport has it that this was an "accident" arranged by the Cleveland Four. Logic would mitigate against this conclusion because it is highly unlikely that the Cleveland Four would compound their difficulties with Schmidt and Lester by taking on the vastly more powerful, Lansky-backed Levinson brothers. However, upon Dennert's death, the Cleveland Four claimed his share of the Flamingo and put one of their operatives in the Flamingo to co-manage the casino with Levinson employees.

TAYLOR AND RIP FARLEY

Unfortunately, however, Lester and Schmidt were not the only sources of trouble in Newport during the 1940s. The Farley brothers posed an even more delicate dilemma. Rip and Taylor Farley were brothers who had come out of the hills of Eastern Kentucky (Clay County) to work in the bootlegging syndicate of the Prohibition era. After the end of Prohibition, Taylor opened a small brothel in Newport, which was not faring as well as he had expected. He went looking for ancillary employment in the casinos and ended up working for "Sleepout" Louis Levinson at the Flamingo. Rip either seriously overestimated his brother's influence or misunderstood the close connections between the Levinsons and Bermans through Meyer Lansky's syndicate because on February 18, 1946, he walked into the Bermans' Yorkshire Club and robbed a dealer of $2,500 at pistol point. Robbing a syndicate casino was obviously not something that would be tolerated in 1940s Newport, and Taylor's association with "Sleepout" Louis was not going to help either of the brothers. On February 22, as Rip and Taylor were leaving the Flamingo, a man in a large black car shot them both with a sawed-off shotgun. Rip died almost immediately, but Taylor, who had been shot in the chest, refused to cooperate and survived the shooting.

The shooter was Danny Meyers (born Aaron Meyervitz). Two days after the Farley shooting, Meyers was found dead, shot in the back of the head, in a parking lot in Pittsburgh in a car stolen from a used car lot in Cincinnati.

Organized crime, contrary to popular perceptions, always prefers to avoid violence because of the attention it brings to day-to-day business. The Farley shootings were no exception. An investigation was initiated, and the Flamingo lost its liquor license. "Sleepout" Louis reopened, serving milk from the bar, at least when state alcohol agents were in town. The license revocation actually saved the syndicate some money in that they simply stopped paying their monthly bribes to the state liquor board inspectors. Taylor Farley fared pretty well, too, considering the situation. He absented himself from Newport for a few years and then returned to work for his fellow Eastern Kentuckians, the Bridewells, at the 345 Club. Apparently, Meyer Lansky's associates were willing to let bygones be bygones.

BUCK BRADY

Another old bootlegger, Buck Brady, was beginning to cause some concern for Sam Tucker representing Cleveland interests in Newport. Buck Brady, yet another of Remus's bootlegging crew, operated the Primrose Club on the road out of Newport toward the Beverly Hills Club for a decade. Brady's management of the Primrose was more than competent. In fact, it was too competent. Brady's club was actually competing with the Cleveland Four's Beverly Hills. Red Masterson, who helped move Pete Schmidt out of the Beverly Hills, was apparently tasked to try to move Brady out of the Primrose. Whether that was to be accomplished by persuasion (after all, Masterson and Brady started their criminal careers together), through a financial offer or through violence has never been made clear. What is clear is that Buck got wind of the syndicate's unhappiness. He struck first on August 5, 1946. Brady lay in wait for Masterson outside the Merchant's Club. As Red was getting into his car, Brady fired a shotgun at him, wounding but not killing Masterson. During his attempted getaway, Brady ran his car into several parked cars and had to flee on foot. The police found Brady hiding in an outhouse and promptly arrested him for disturbing the peace.

In the spirit of true organized crime camaraderie, Masterson refused to identify Brady as the shooter at his trial, and George Remus showed up as a character witness for Buck. The disturbing the peace charge was quickly dropped. The Cleveland Four saw no reason to prolong the incident with another public act of violence. They told Brady to leave Newport or be killed. Wisely, Brady retired to Florida after giving the Primrose to the Cleveland Four as a peace offering. The Cleveland Four renamed the club the Latin Quarter, remodeled and expanded it. Dave Whitfield, one of the suspected arsonists from the Beverly Hills Club fire, was given the job of manager after his release from prison. Whitfield's parole had been arranged for "considerations." The Cleveland Four transferred $7,000 in cash and a prize bull to a state official for help in speeding along Whitfield's rehabilitation.

BOOKMAKING AND LAYOFF BANKING

Casino gambling wasn't the only source of gambling profits for organized crime in 1940s Newport. Bookmaking was a major organized crime enterprise nationwide, and Newport became a center for organized crime "layoff" banks. A layoff bank operates as a kind of insurance company for illegal bookmakers. Bookies, who are getting too much betting action on a particular fight, horse race or sporting events, sell some of their betting action to larger, better-financed "layoff" banks. The layoff bank divides the risk with the bookie and also, of course, divides the profits with the bookies, all for a fee or handling charge.

An important layoff bank, which covered much of the betting action in the Midwest, was located at Fourth and York Streets. The "Bobben

Realty Company" was run by the Lasoff brothers, Bob and Ben, or as they were known locally, "Big Porky" and "Little Porky," and their partner Nig Devine. Devine was also a major Newport caterer, who provided casinos and restaurants with pre-prepared food. Layoff banks are inevitably connected with larger syndicates and form the primary basis for profit-taking in bookmaking for organized crime syndicates. In the case of the Lasoff brothers and Nig Devine, their layoff book was a creation of Meyer Lansky's New York Syndicate.

In the late 1940s, Gil "the Brain" Beckley would take over the Bobben Realty layoff bank in partnership with Eddie Levinson. Under Beckley's leadership, federal law enforcement officials would later allege, Bobben Realty grew into the largest layoff bank in the country.

Screw Andrews

Screw Andrews (born Frank Andriola) started his criminal career as a moonshiner in the suburbs of Cincinnati. Later, he moved on to the numbers rackets, primarily in African American neighborhoods. By the mid-1940s, along with his brother, "Spider," and his nephew, "Junior," Screw owned several liquor stores and newspaper stands across the river in Newport. Through those otherwise legitimate businesses, Screw was able to expand his numbers syndicate into Newport. In the late 1940s, Andrews decided to move against African American–owned casinos in Newport. Making use of a well-placed bribe, Andrews was able to convince Newport police to raid Steve Payne's Sportsman's Club on May 14, 1947. In 1948, Payne was murdered, and Andrews purchased the Sportsman's Club from the Newport redevelopment authority. The Sportsman's Club was now the headquarters of Andrews's numbers racket and casino operations.

In 1952, Screw acquired ownership of the Alibi Club, another African American gambling venue. Screw accomplished the takeover in his typical violent style. On January 13, 1952, a shootout occurred at the Alibi club. Melvin Clark, the major remaining African American competitor of Andrews in the numbers racket, shot and killed Andrews's casino manager, who pulled a gun on Clark. Andrews sensed an opportunity to move on Clark's rackets, especially if Clark was convicted of murder in the shooting. But Newport, being Newport, dealt with shootings in a more benevolent manner. Clark was found guilty not of assault or murder, but of carrying a concealed weapon. He was sentenced to eighteen months' probation and told to stay out of Newport for that period. Screw Andrews had a very limited window of opportunity to make his move on Clark's rackets.

Clark returned to Newport in 1954 and immediately opened a new casino, the Coconut Grove, a club that would directly compete with Screw Andrews's interests. Screw ended the threat by shooting Clark and killing him. He was charged with murder, but was assisted by the fact that police didn't even investigate the crime. He pled self-defense and was acquitted.

Screw Andrews may have been successful at avoiding murder charges, but unlike his syndicate counterparts, who were very careful to always pay federal income taxes on their profits and meet the requirement of the Federal Wagering Stamp Act, Screw was a bit more cavalier in dealing with the Treasury Department. Later, after the cleanup of Newport, he was convicted on tax charges and sent to federal prison for six years.

THE KEFAUVER COMMITTEE

The specter of reform in Newport was actually raised not in Newport itself, but hundreds of miles away in Washington, D.C., where Senator Estes Kefauver's Committee to Investigate Organized Crime in Interstate Commerce started to hold hearings.

Newport came to the attention of the Kefauver Committee during its public hearing in Cleveland when testimony revealed that the Cleveland Syndicate had acquired interests in Northern Kentucky casinos, as well as in Nevada, Michigan and, to some extent, in Florida. However, the local officials from Newport who appeared before the Kefauver Committee demonstrated that they were satisfied with the status quo.

On the stand and under oath during the nationally televised hearings, Newport Police Chief Gugel responded that he had never visited a gambling house in his city. At the Kefauver hearing, Chief Gugel was represented by none other than attorney Charles Lester. When asked if he knew that Cincinnati newspapers advertised gambling places in Newport, the chief replied that he never read Cincinnati papers. When he was asked if he was "the only man in the entire vicinity who didn't know that any taxi driver could take you to a selection of five or six gambling joints," he replied, "I never ride in a taxi."

Commonwealth Attorney William Wise also demonstrated a lackadaisical attitude toward Newport gambling and the individuals involved. When asked if he knew Morris Kleinman, Louis Rothkopf and Moe Dalitz, who were partners in the Beverly Hills Club, he said he had never heard of them. Wise did say that he had sought indictments against several gamblers who had run the Beverly Hills Club and several other gambling casinos. However, he and the commonwealth attorney for Kenton County testified that the gamblers closed down regularly when the county grand juries were meeting. This allowed for the juries to say they were unable to find any existing gambling. Wise added that when some gamblers were indicted, they had been acquitted or had the charges against them reduced to misdemeanors with small fines. The chief counsel for the committee read into the IRS records that the Beverly Hills Club had showed net profits of $426,199 in 1948 and 1949.

Campbell County Judge Ray Murphy and Kenton County Judge Joseph Gooedenough testified that they always charged the grand juries to investigate gambling, but the juries never brought felony indictments. Malcolm Rhodes, Newport's city manager, told the committee that before he took office the city had been issuing brokerage licenses to bookmakers ranging from $350 to $8,090 a year, depending on the size of the operation. The money, under the guise of a payroll tax, went into the city treasury. Campbell County Sheriff Ray Diebold was criticized for allowing a "flagrant breakdown of law enforcement in Campbell County." The committee further stated that the sheriff seemed to regard tax collection as his only duty and read him the Kentucky law describing his duties, which stated that "a Sheriff must visit every tavern, dance hall and similar establishments once a month and cannot deputize anyone to make the inspection." The sheriff responded that he had only learned of that three weeks ago and had not had time to comply with it. The combined weight of the testimony revealed that gambling was well known to all the public officials, but none of them was serious about taking any action.

The impact of the Kefauver Committee hearings on Newport was immediate. It was clear to some citizens that something had to be done after the national revelations on TV and in the print media. But it would be done in typical Newport fashion.

REFORM SYNDICATE STYLE

Attempts at reform came slowly in Newport. In the early 1950s, a group of clergymen in neighboring Kenton County hired Assistant Attorney General Jesse Lewis to investigate political corruption in Covington and

Kenton County. Lewis filed suit against the Kenton County commonwealth attorney, alleging that he was engaged in nonfeasance with regard to the gambling laws. The judge hearing the lawsuit agreed and began disbarment proceedings against the commonwealth attorney.

On March 7, 1952, the state police raided the Lookout House located in Kenton County. They seized $20,000 in gambling equipment and arrested casino employees and patrons alike. The Cleveland Four made a quick decision. The Lookout House would not reopen. It was better to sacrifice one establishment to protect the others across the river in Newport, where state police interference was not likely to be tolerated. Jimmy Brink had not been present during the raid, so he had not been arrested. But his lucky streak was at an end. Brink, an accomplished pilot, died on August 6, 1952, while flying himself to Miami.

In Newport, the reform movement actually was better organized and more powerful. There was a good reason for that. Reform came to Newport courtesy of the Cleveland Four. Red Masterson, fully recovered from the Brady shooting, started meeting with local businessmen. Out of these consultations came the Newport Civic Association (NCA), which would raise the issue of gambling and prostitution, and field candidates for office, under the slogan of "Clean Up, Not Close Up." The moderate businessmen recruited by Masterson were swayed by a longstanding tradition in Newport's history—closing the casinos would hurt business. A Newport businessman reportedly made the comment, "Clean up this place and what have we got? A big plenty o' nothing. Just plain nothing."

With the syndicate's bankroll funding the campaign, the Newport-style reformers swept the elections. And business continued. Peter Schmidt was still trying to build a gambling empire. Despite the election results, which put syndicate-backed reformers in office, Schmidt went ahead with a new project. Schmidt probably misread some events and thought there was an ongoing Cleveland Syndicate disengagement from Newport. Sam Tucker had moved to Miami in 1949 to oversee gambling interests in Broward County and Havana. Moe Dalitz had purchased the Desert Inn in Las Vegas from Wilbur Clark and seemed to be devoting his entire attention to that project. So Schmidt built yet another casino at 18 East Fifth Street, called the Glenn Schmidt Playtorium. The Playtorium was a one-story building with a restaurant, cocktail lounge, bowling alley and a basement casino. However, the Cleveland Syndicate was still well represented in Newport through their newly elected reform government. The "reformers" thought Schmidt's opening of the Playtorium was just another act of defiance on his part. The Newport Civic Association members ordered a raid on Schmidt.

Schmidt's ally, Charles Lester, retaliated by arranging a raid on the Cleveland Four's Merchants Club. Lester found a detective named Jack Thiem willing to take charge of the raid. Thiem's exact role in the Newport drama is unclear. Some sources believe he was a corrupt cop on Lester's payroll. Others believe he was an impeccably honest officer simply doing his duty. In any event, following the Farley shootings, Thiem was selected to head up a gangster unit in the police department. In that role, he had gathered evidence and compiled dossiers for years waiting for any sign of reform to show its face in Newport. With the success of the NCA, Theim apparently believed his day had come. He was not entirely correct in that assessment.

On occasion, even the cleverest organized crime scheme can overreach. The NCA had come to power with the direct assistance of the Cleveland Four. With the attack on Schmidt, apparently someone felt the reformers' work was done. In the 1952 election, the word was put out that the NCA slate of candidates was to be reelected. Whoever made that call was not counting well because in the November election the Lester-Schmidt candidate for mayor, Robert Siddell, the street minstrel, won. Once again, Peter Schmidt would overreach his opportunity. Schmidt approached Jack Thiem and made him an offer. He suggested that Thiem serve as official police "enforcer" for the "new" regime. Schmidt was proposing, in a straightforward manner, that he and Lester, with Thiem's assistance, would take over organized crime in Newport. Whether out of a sense of duty and impeccable honesty, because of conflicting underworld loyalties or because he didn't think Schmidt and Lester could pull it off, Thiem did precisely the opposite. He launched a major raid on Peter Schmidt's Playtorium. At that time, the detective division operated independently of the rest of the police force. Thiem found Chief Gugel and three other detectives present in the casino. This was especially interesting since, as was mentioned earlier, several years before, in his appearance before the Kefauver Committee, Chief Gugel had denied knowing of any gambling going on in Newport. A photographer from the *Louisville Courier-Journal*, along at Thiem's invitation, took a picture of the chief. He was promptly arrested, and his film was destroyed.

The logistics of this raid are interesting, and the potential implications to understanding organized crime in Newport are compelling. First, this was a very expensive raid. Thiem chose not to use Newport police, but rather hired a busload of detectives from Louisville to conduct the raid. The detectives were deputized on the bus while traveling to Newport because they obviously had no jurisdiction in Newport. Someone had to fund the raid, and that someone was not local or county government. Second, this was a logistically complex action that required careful planning and information about individuals in Louisville and their level of trustworthiness that seems, at least on its face, beyond Jack Thiem. But such an expensive and complex operation was not beyond the Cleveland Syndicate or the individuals associated with Meyer Lansky. It may be that Thiem approached either, or both, of these syndicates for help. It may be that the Cleveland Four were annoyed with whoever had made the decisions to dump the NCA candidates in the election, probably Red Masterson, and were simply taking corrective measures. It may be that individuals associated with the Levinsons and Bermans, representing

WHY WON'T PUBLIC OFFICIALS ACT?

A federal grand jury, convened during the March term 1953 at Covington, suggests some possible answers to the question posed in this section:

> *It is not apparent from any of the testimony heard before us that there has been any effort on the part of the local police of Newport or the County Patrol or the Sheriff of Campbell County to enforce the Kentucky statutes against gambling and vice. It is not apparent from any of the testimony heard before us that there has been any effort on the part of the Commonwealth's Attorney, County Attorney or City Attorney of Newport to do anything whatsoever to carry out their duties to enforce the law, violations of which are apparent to any residents of the county. These officers when testifying before this jury said that they had done all in their power to investigate or cause investigations to be made of violations of the gambling laws and that they had been unable to ascertain evidence of gambling in the city or county.*
>
> *The inescapable conclusion is forced upon this jury as a result of this probe that there must be some reason why duly elected and sworn officials of Newport and Campbell County fail to perform their duties. There must be some connection between the gambling interests and these officials which could cause them to neglect their duties over such a long time. Either they believe that vice and gambling are not immoral [sic], or that it is good for the community; or they have become friendly to it or some other reason.*

Lansky's interests, were less than impressed with the deterioration in the political climate of Newport and acted on their own. Whatever happened, and why it happened, resulted in an outcome that was not good for anyone.

Thiem's deputized raiders were arrested by Chief Gugel. Thiem was also arrested on a wide range of charges and taken into custody. Screw Andrews approached Theim and offered to make the charges go away if Thiem would leave Newport. But Thiem, either believing he had some form of protection or still believing in the credibility of Newport's criminal justice system, chose to stand trial. That was another poor choice. The trial was a legal lynching. The ever-present Charles Lester, who had no standing in front of the court, was allowed to participate in the trial, making motions, questioning witnesses and addressing the jury. The judge was clearly hostile to Thiem, and a string of witnesses perjured themselves. Thiem avoided serving time in prison by finally leaving Newport. Perhaps a clue to the mystery of what had actually happened during this confusing and complex series of events can be found in Thiem's exit. He went to Las Vegas and took a security job with Ed Levinson at the Sands Casino.

Despite the miscalculations and the diverted attention of the Cleveland Four to their other projects, organized crime was still percolating along quite nicely in Newport. Clergy in Newport, somewhat encouraged by the successes of their brethren in Covington, started to organize against gambling in the mid-1950s. But the Newport clergy couldn't even annoy casino operators. They gathered "evidence," which after all was not very hard to come by, on illegal gambling; they picketed in front of the casinos; and a few of the more adventurous actually entered the casinos for a little tableside preaching. No one was paying much attention, and most of the ministerial efforts were sources of derision.

RENEWED NATIONAL ATTENTION

Newport was again to receive national attention. A 1957 article appearing in *Esquire* magazine called Newport "Sin Town" and Cincinnati's playground, with houses of bordellos, bust-out joints and plush nightlife. The article reported that "sin" was Newport's major industry, drawing in an estimated one million patrons who spent $30 million a year on gambling and women. The author said that $1 million of the $30 million went to payoffs. The Cincinnati taxi driver who took the author to Newport reported: "I'll take you to an on-the-level gambling house run by the Cleveland Syndicate, but if it's women you want, you'd better get a Newport taxi to take you to a house. I don't want to get mixed up in interstate stuff." The same taxi driver cautioned against visiting bust-out joints:

> *You ain't been here before, have you? Just don't let 'em [Newport taxis] steer you into a bust-out joint. Brother, if you get into one of them places they'll turn you upside down and shake you good to be sure you got nothin' left before they let you out.*

The author closed the article with a quote from a local resident:

> *The civic fabric of Newport is rotten, but that is what the majority of its voters want…*[Responding to the role of the women in the community] *The better class will not get themselves involved. They are active in the P.T.A. and charitable organizations, but they will not buck the vice overlords. Perhaps they are afraid their families will be hurt. Or maybe, they realize that some of their husbands' business prosperity comes indirectly from the money spent on vice. The fact is that much of our economy is dependent on vice and the majority of our people would rather have the money than get rid of this reputation as America's most wicked city.*

RENEWED REFORM EFFORTS

Whether or not it was in response to the new publicity, by 1958 the clergy had helped to organize the Social Action Committee (SAC). In October 1958, the SAC would go to the Campbell County grand jury with evidence of gambling. Members of the SAC had investigated the existence of the casinos, bust-out joints and whorehouses; they came to the grand jury with locations and names. After all, the Kefauver Committee, national magazines and the advertisements in local newspapers pointed out where they were. And every taxi driver in Cincinnati or Newport knew where they were. If you still could not find them, you could walk downtown and look at their flamboyant neon signs. However, the "deck was stacked" against them. The commonwealth attorney was William Wise, who didn't know anything before the Kefauver Committee, and the circuit judge was Ray Murphy, who had come to office shortly after the Cleveland Syndicate had taken control of the Beverly Hills Country Club from Peter Schmidt. Several ministers and

Hank Messick, a reporter from the *Louisville Courier-Journal*, testified before the grand jury. Messick's car had sugar put in its tank, and he claimed to have been poisoned before his appearance before the grand jury. Messick actually showed his "sweetened" fuel pump to the jurors. Later, prior to an appearance before another grand jury, Messick claimed that an attempt was made on his life. The grand jury refused to indict, even though several jury officials asked for indictments. The majority remained firmly opposed. However, the grand jury, in its final report, suggested a more stringent program of law enforcement because of a "laxity in law enforcement with regards to the operation of taverns, prostitution, and gaming." Surprisingly, even though no indictments were returned, the grand jury stated that if law authorities were unable to handle the situation, state police should be invited in to assist. After all, there was the pervasive feeling that Newport would become a ghost city without its attractions, and the residents of Cincinnati across the river needed a place to drink and relax.

In February 1959, SAC tried again, presenting still more evidence to the grand jury. The jurors were openly hostile to the clergy and other SAC members, and they issued a report that they could find no gambling or other vice anywhere in Newport. They were suffering from a peculiar eye condition common to grand juries and public officials in Newport for almost three decades. The affliction, known as "Newport Eye," prevented public officials and grand juries from seeing gambling and vice in their midst. But as the 1950s were ending, the management of vice was less efficient than before, as the major syndicate operatives went elsewhere, and the declining profits were weakening community resolve to preserve vice. The SAC raised sufficient funds to hire an attorney and prepared for yet another attack on organized vice. The reformers were set to take advantage of Newport's national reputation as Kentucky's Sin City and political and citizen apathy.

TIMES THEY ARE A-CHANGING

It is not at all surprising that little public or political support for closing down organized crime could be found in Newport. Restaurant, gas station, tavern and hotel owners all believed that without gambling and prostitution no one would come to Newport, and they would be driven out of business. Most local merchants did the majority of their business at night, when the casinos and brothels were flourishing. In fact, Newport was one of the few cities outside of Las Vegas that was open all night. While merchants' concerns were no doubt valid, they were also overstated. Time and progress had passed Newport by.

First, in the 1930s and 1940s, travel was limited to the automobiles and trains that brought the casino and brothel patrons to Newport. By the mid-1950s, planes were more common, and travel across larger distances was more convenient. In the 1930s and 1940s, Las Vegas was still an undeveloped gambling Mecca, and Havana had not yet been refurbished with New York mob money.

Second, the demography of America was changing. In the 1930s and 1940s, the population was situated in such a way that Newport was within eight hours' travel time of about two-thirds of every adult living in the United States. By the mid-1950s, strange and exotic locales like Florida, Arizona and California were attracting more people. The population base was shifting, and that shift made Newport a far less attractive organized crime venue.

Finally, the syndicates had moved, and they were paying less attention to Newport, even to their own properties in Newport. The Cleveland Four were no longer concentrated in Newport, but in Havana and Las Vegas. Moe Dalitz was supervising the construction of the brand-new Stardust in Las Vegas, and Louis Rothkopf committed suicide in 1956, mourning the death of his wife in 1955. Lansky and his New York City partners were in Florida, Cuba, Nevada, Arizona and getting ready to enter the Bahamas. Ed Levinson and the Bermans were in Las Vegas, and Sleepout Louis was trying to figure out where Nassau, the Bahamas, was—his next management assignment. To continue to flourish, organized crime in Newport needed to change. It did, but not for the better.

At least for the moment, illegal casino gambling was still the only game in town. The Stork Club became the Silver Slipper and then the Stardust, probably as a result of a Cleveland Four takeover from Marshal Jim Harris when the latter went to prison for pandering. Two Monmouth Street casinos changed names. The Kid Able Club became Monmouth Cigar, a tobacco shop with gambling in the back. The new small casino called the Spotted Calf, which was actually more of a lunch counter than a gambling location, opened at Fifth and York Streets. A small club, the Congo, which was primarily a nightclub with some gambling action, opened up on Central Avenue. The Congo was frequented by African American patrons. The Glenn Schmidt Playtorium was still operating, but it was no longer a casino. The bowling and restaurant parts of the business were doing so well that Schmidt didn't want the business closed down because of gambling. He moved the casino operation next door to 12 East Fifth Street, into a business he called the Snax

Bar. His old compatriot, Robert Siddell, turned out of the mayor's office by a syndicate-backed candidate, was the manager at the Snax Bar. Peter Schmidt died of natural causes in 1958, and attorney Charles Lester took over the Playtorium and the Snax Bar. The old Glenn Rendezvous had been taken over by a local operative, Tito Carinici. Carinici's Glenn Rendezvous was frequented by Frank Sinatra and Dean Martin. Carinici, a small-time scam operator for the most part, was not up to the task of managing a major gambling operation, as his later mistakes would make clear.

Part Four

THE GANGLAND
GONG SHOW

As Newport entered the 1960s, there were clear signs that the three-decade-long gambling boom was coming to a close. While the major syndicates still had holdings in Newport, the leadership was gone. The talent for political manipulation, attracting high rollers and maintaining the uninterrupted, predictable, daily operation of vice was now in Las Vegas and the Bahamas. The local players were scrambling to maintain profitability.

The Glenn Rendezvous had been a successful gambling venue since the 1940s. It was even advertised as a hotel, but the rooms were for customers, not guests. Under the management of Tito Carinci, gambling revenue was falling markedly. Carinci turned the Glenn Rendezvous into a high-class bust-out joint. Even taxi drivers were steering customers away from the club. However, Tito, without the benefit of syndicate guidance or stabilizing influence, reacted to falling revenue by changing the primary product of the club, while still retaining gambling action. He added a strip show downstairs and replaced the bookmaking operation on the third floor—the most profitable, but also the most complex, of the gambling enterprises—with prostitutes. He renamed the Glen Rendezvous the Tropicana, in deference to "Doc" Stacher's Las Vegas casino, and put a large neon sign featuring nude women in the window. What was happening to the Glenn Rendezvous was symptomatic of what was happening to Newport.

THE TIDE BEGINS TO TURN

The SAC was still actively seeking indictments against the gamblers. Their run of bad luck came to an end when Campbell County Judge Murphy, who was supposed to preside over the fall session of the grand jury, fell ill and was replaced by a judge from another county. That judge was Edward J. Hill, who as a circuit judge in Harlan had gained the reputation as "the tamer of Bloody Harlan." The new judge dissolved the old grand jury, convened a special grand jury on November 10, 1960, and ordered the destruction of some long-confiscated slot machines on the steps of the courthouse.

The vice operators and public officials sensed trouble. They were determined that the tamer of Bloody Harlan wasn't going to get his chance to reform Newport. In a desperate move to stop the investigation, Judge Murphy, the original judge, still ill, climbed out of bed and returned to take charge of the new grand jury. But the composition of the grand jury had changed, and Judge Murphy could not stop the investigation. The maverick jurors told the commonwealth attorney to get lost and began their own investigation. The SAC put on its witnesses, and in an unheard-of development for Newport, the grand jury indicted Campbell County Sheriff Norbert Roll for nonfeasance. Sheriff Roll had the audacity to deny that gambling existed in the county, contradicting the testimony of the county judge and county attorney, both of whom acknowledged its existence but denied responsibility. The grand jury had no choice but to indict the sheriff when he denied there was gambling. Commonwealth Attorney William Wise returned to the jury room and tried to talk them out of the sheriff's indictment. He cited the trouble it would cause, but they did not relent.

The sheriff's trial was to begin on December 6, 1960, and with local prosecutors and judges now in charge, Newport would return to its normal way of doing business. The gambling joints closed during the sheriff's trial, supposedly so he could swear that there was no gambling in Newport. The prosecutor barely went through the motions of presenting evidence against the sheriff, although *Courier-Journal* reporter Hank Messick was able to introduce betting tickets, casino gambling chips and casino matchbooks. The sheriff at first claimed he didn't know of any gambling and could not make arrests for things he didn't know, and then he added that even if there was gambling it was unfair to single him out for blame. It took the jury twelve minutes to acquit him. They would have returned their verdict sooner, but it took a few minutes to find the judge. Where a year earlier such a decision would be met with laughter and jokes in the community, this time more and more residents were becoming convinced that their city and county were corrupt anachronisms, out of step with the times. The feeling among the reformers was that the gamblers had won a victory but lost the war. Later events would prove them right.

The SAC and the clergy were particularly outraged at the sheriff's acquittal. They declared February 12, 1961, United Sunday and set out to raise enough in contributions that day to continue the investigation. Their first step was to present affidavits asking for the removal of Campbell County officials, including Circuit Judge Ray Murphy, County Judge Andrew Jolly, Newport Mayor Ralph Mussman, Newport Police Chief George Gugel, Campbell County Police Chief Harry Stewart and Sheriff Norbert Roll. The governor demurred and declined to act at that time. The Campbell County grand jury, now under control of the traditional political powers, countered with a diatribe, written by Commonwealth Attorney Wise, against the reformers and outside newspapers:

> *We are mindful of a continuing campaign being carried out by a reform group which has enjoyed the active assistance of newspapers published in Louisville. As representative citizens who consider ourselves decent, law-abiding people, we feel impelled to assert that this group, essentially devoted to reform, has caused a grossly distorted picture of our community to be presented to the various news media. Those who manufacture news through public pontifications likewise thrive on the publicity that they thus enjoy.*

The diatribe went on to say that "a community in many ways chooses its way of life as do individuals," and if a change was needed it could be accomplished by vote, ignoring the fact that the gamblers and vice operators controlled the political system and exerted undue influence on the system of voting. Wise had gone too far. A salesman living in Fort Thomas began holding meetings with people interested in doing something about the situation in Newport and the obvious corruption among elected officials. The reform movement had started.

COMMITTEE OF 500

The reform movement got a major assist when some local businessmen, suffering from the decline in vice business, which had been supporting them, formed the Committee of 500. The committee eventually had twenty-five hundred members. Its purpose was to find and support men and women of unquestioned honesty and integrity for public office. The Committee of 500 had some advantages over past reform efforts. First, it was religiously nonsectarian and therefore would not be beset by religious divisions. Second, it was nonpartisan, thus avoiding political divisions. And third, it was well financed. The committee decided on three goals: to mobilize public support against gambling, to press the governor to remove public officials who failed to enforce the law and to nominate reform candidates for local offices. They chose four candidates to run for Newport city commission offices. However, the reformers decided that the best and easiest way to deal with the situation was to support an independent candidate for Campbell County sheriff. The sheriff, operating out of Newport, would be in a key position to get rid of the gambling and vice. The committee created a new Switch to Honesty Party, with prominent lawyer and reformer Henry Cook as counsel, and chose a dynamic and charismatic leader in the form of George Ratterman to run for sheriff.

George Ratterman, a well-known personality, lived outside of Newport in Fort Thomas, a fairly affluent suburb, also the home of Attorney Charles Lester, Red Masterson and most of the members of the Committee of 500. Ratterman's family had ties to the area—his brother was a priest and the dean of men at Xavier University. His two brothers-in-law were attorneys, and his father-in-law was president of the Newport National Bank. His in-laws had been involved in the formation of the Committee of 500. Ratterman was a happily married man with a beautiful wife and eight children. In his college days, he had been an all-American football player at Notre Dame and later went to the pros, playing with Buffalo, New York, Montreal and Cleveland. He played for the Cleveland Browns as backup to the legendary Otto Graham. During the off seasons, Ratterman went to law school, taking ten years to earn his law degree. He was also an investment banker and a professional sportscaster, doing weekly football commentaries. However, he had no law enforcement experience.

Ratterman's Catholic background brought with him the support of the bishop of Covington. Bishop Richard H. Ackerman condemned prostitution and drunkenness and added that for gambling to be morally permissible it would have to be legal. The bishop's actions brought many Catholics into the reform movement. The lack of Catholic support had, in the past, prevented a united front against the gamblers and vice operators. Ratterman expressed his willingness to run in the following remarks:

> *I am willing to run for office if you people are really serious. I am not willing to sacrifice four years of my life if this is to be but a temporary*

clamor. There have been reform movements in our county before. They did not last. That is the reason this county is in the mess which we all know exists today. We must not let that happen again.

I have eight children. I don't want them to grow up in a community where syndicated gambling finds a home, where prostitution flourishes, where officials are known to be corrupt, and where now the illegal narcotics industry has found a home.

Ratterman was well aware of the potential for trouble in his decision to run: "I'm told that if I run for sheriff, I will probably be the victim of all kinds of slanderous attacks. If that is the price one must pay to run for office as your candidate, so be it."

Ratterman and a group of supporters traveled to Frankfort to meet with Governor Combs, who promised his support if the people of Newport cooperated with him. He did promise to send ABC agents to look for gambling on any premises that had a liquor license. This disappointed the reformers because it was well known that the casinos sold liquor without a license. Nevertheless, the reform movement was riding high—but the gamblers and vice operators were not finished.

THE GONG SHOW

The local gamblers tried to control the Committee of 500 in much the same way the Cleveland Four had controlled the Newport Civic Association in the early 1950s. Red Masterson was among the charter members of the reform group. But with Ratterman's ascension to leadership, Red had to report that the committee was beyond control. The ability to forge common ground, which Sam Tucker and Moe Dalitz had used to blunt earlier reform efforts, was beyond Red Masterson's more limited talents. Attorney Charles Lester stepped forward to try to organize the opposition to Ratterman. Lester, by now, was reportedly the "brains" behind most of the legal maneuvering protecting the illegal operations in Newport. The FBI had reports that Attorney Lester was depositing Newport gambling money in Swiss banks on tours to Europe.

There were three gambling and vice factions in Newport at the time. First, the Cleveland Syndicate operated the Beverly Hills, the Merchant's Club and the Yorkshire Club, but their leaders and real money-making operations were by this time in Las Vegas. Albert "Red" Masterson was their representative and enforcer, but he could not control the new reform movement. The second faction was the independents represented by Tito Carinci at the Flamingo, the owners of the Playtorium and the Snax Bar and attorney Charles Lester. The third faction was the prostitution rackets and the numbers in Newport and Cincinnati. The group was dominated by the killer Screw Andrews. It was up to the conniving Lester and the not-so-bright Carinci to come up with a plan.

Lester and Tito Carinci came up with what turned out to be a very bad idea. They would blackmail or smear Ratterman before the election, thereby either turning him against reform or assuring his defeat. What better way to derail the reformers than to expose their candidate as a hypocrite? It was a tactic that had been successful before. In 1950, a local clergyman, who was part of a reform movement, was drugged and photographed in his shorts with a scantily clad girl on his lap. The clergyman left town in a hurry.

On May 8, 1961, Ratterman got a message through a friend, Tom Paisley, from Tito Carinci. It seemed that Tito wanted to quit organized crime and join the "good guys." Ratterman and Carnici had been friends through their football associations for years.

THE OFFICIAL VERSION

According to the police report, at 2:32 a.m. on May 9, 1961, an unknown person called police headquarters and asked to speak to Detective Pat Ciafardini. Detective Ciafardini, it would later be discovered, was not on duty at the time. He had stopped by headquarters after returning from a Fraternal Order of Police meeting in Bowling Green, Kentucky. The report informed the officer in charge that prostitution was going on at the Glenn Hotel. Caifardini called in a patrol car containing Detectives Upshire White and Joseph Quitter to accompany him to the hotel to investigate the complaint. The report said that when the three officers entered the lobby, they were stopped by Tito Carinci. The officers arrested Carinci and took him up to Room 314, supposedly the location of the anonymous prostitution complaint.

In Room 314, the report states, the officers found "one April Flowers, female, white, age 26, alias Juanita Jean Hodges, particularly [sic] clothes seated on a bed in the room, a robe pulled up around her waist and one George William Ratterman, age 38 years." The report goes on to say that Ratterman was only wearing a white shirt and a pair of socks. Ratterman allegedly jumped from the bed and shoved Ciafardini, who in turn shoved him back on the bed. Ratterman then "donned a light blue green Chinelle [*sic*] bed spread and he, Flowers, and Carinci were brought to this office." At police headquarters, Flowers was charged with engaging in prostitution; Carinci was charged with breach of the peace. The reform candidate for sheriff, George Ratterman, was charged with breach of the peace, disorderly conduct and resisting arrest.

ALL HELL BREAKS LOOSE

The arrest caused a local media frenzy. It made regional news. The arrest also piqued national interest, U.S. Attorney General Robert Kennedy was informed of it almost immediately. He had had his eyes on Newport since the 1950s Kefauver hearings. The next day, Ronald Goldfarb from the Justice Department was on his way to Kentucky. TV cameras and representatives from Cincinnati and Kentucky newspapers were present at the police press conference, where the official police report was distributed and Ciafardini explained what happened. Carinci and other sources close to the gamblers told reporters that Ratterman was a frequent customer and a sexual degenerate who regularly made use of the services of prostitutes. The setup was so crude that it took only a matter of hours for it to unravel and for "all hell to break loose." As one longtime Newport bookmaker told columnist Jimmy Breslin, as soon as he heard what happened he remarked, "Some stupid sonofabitch thought this one up...We're going to have a mess on account of this." He was right. Breslin wrote that "before the ink was dry in the police blotter, Newport's status quo as a great gambling town was dead."

Several hours after his release from jail, Ratterman's wife took him to see their family physician because he was still groggy and incoherent. The family physician rushed him to the hospital for blood and urine samples. The samples were sent to Dr. Frank Cleveland, a pathologist from the Kittering Laboratories and the pathologist for the coroner in Cincinnati and Newport. Dr. Cleveland found large traces of chloral hydrate in Ratterman's blood. Chloral hydrate, or the "Mickey Finn," had been used for a long time in the bust-out joints in Newport. It induces sleep and can cause confusion and a lack of clear judgment. Later in the morning, Ratterman gave the following statement:

I was drugged last night and awakened in the bedroom of the apartment of Tito Carinci at the Glenn Hotel in Newport…I was so groggy and weak I could hardly lift my arms. I was pushed to the floor several times. I recall seeing a woman with the men in the room where I was awakened. I have no idea who she was and had never seen her before. The officers refused several requests to return my trousers and I was taken to the police station wrapped in bed covering…

I have known Tito Carinci for a long time, from the days when we were both playing football…Since I announced my candidacy for sheriff he has approached a mutual friend [Tom Paisley] *on several occasions and has mentioned the fact that he would like to talk to me…Yesterday our mutual friend mentioned to me that Tito was very anxious to talk to me. I said that I did not believe that Tito's place of business was a good meeting ground but would consent to talk to him in Cincinnati yesterday evening in the Terrace Hilton Hotel.*

The gangster and bookmaker Gil Beckley was with Carinci when they met, but the law enforcement amateur Ratterman didn't know who he was. Beckley left as soon as they showed up.

Carinci suggested we come to his place of business and be his guests for dinner.

I mentioned again that I did not believe his place of business was a proper one in which I should be seen. He said that he lived over his place of business and suggested that we could get to his room unnoticed through a back door and eat in complete privacy.

This was obviously the wrong place to go as I should have realized. Nevertheless the three of us did go to his suite…Shortly thereafter I suddenly became quite groggy and stretched out on a bed in the bedroom. I recall nothing more until I was awakened by the commotion.

Ratterman's arrest and alleged frame-up was now national news. The national coverage heightened the interest of Attorney General Robert Kennedy. Within hours of being notified, Kennedy had sent thirty-nine FBI agents to Newport. Newport would become Kennedy's primary target in the war on organized crime. Public opinion swung decidedly in favor of the reformers. The citizens of Newport recognized a frame-up when they saw it, and they had seen plenty. This time, they would do something about it. A statement issued by the Newport Ministerial Association captured the mood of the community.

Kentucky's Sin City

We, the Newport Ministerial Association, believe that George Ratterman was framed, the victim of a malicious plot, by members of the local underworld who are seeking to defame his reputation and discredit the movement to clean up Newport and Campbell County. In light of this development, we unanimously affirm our intention to support George Ratterman's candidacy for Campbell County Sheriff.

But Charles Lester and the Newport police were undeterred. Ratterman's trial on prostitution charges began on May 16. Media interest was nationwide. Magazines such as *Time* were present. The *New York Times* was represented. National live TV coverage was provided at each recess. Reporters sat on the floor and in the jury box. Among those taking notes in the courtroom were two of the thirty-nine FBI agents dispatched to Newport. There was an overflow crowd of three hundred people in the seventy-five-seat courtroom. Newport had never seen such a trial in police court before or since.

Henry Cook, the Committee of 500 and Ratterman's lawyer could have gotten Ratterman off without a trial on a legal technicality. The arrest was legally improper. The officers had made a misdemeanor arrest without a warrant on the basis of an anonymous tip. However, this would have left Ratterman looking guilty, only released on a legal technicality. For that matter, Charles Lester, the lawyer for both Tito Carinci and April Flowers, could have gotten his clients off on the same basis, but that would have disturbed his plans to smear Ratterman and derail his bid for sheriff.

In a move to ensure maximum damage to Ratterman's reputation, Lester persuaded the judge to have Carinci's and Flower's cases heard first, thereby ensuring that the sordid accusations against Ratterman would be heard. Carinci, April Flowers, a recently appointed Kentucky colonel and the arresting officer, Detective Ciafardini, testified, each giving what would later be determined to be perjured testimony. Detective Ciafardini, in an effort to prove his truthfulness, asked God to strike him dead if he was not telling the truth. Carnici, Catholic like Ratterman, stated that he had gone to church that morning, knelt before the altar and swore that his statement was true. He then challenged Ratterman to do the same. On the same day that the prosecution witnesses were testifying against Ratterman, Robert Kennedy was testifying before Congress on the need for new legislation to fight organized crime. Attorney General Kennedy was using Newport, Kentucky, as a prime example of a wide-open city:

There is wide-open gambling in Newport, Kentucky, adjacent to Cincinnati, Ohio and Covington, Kentucky. A review of the financial statements of 4

Newport gambling casinos in 1957 revealed that 11 persons, who reside outside of Kentucky, participated in the casino profits.

Ratterman's attorney had no need for the histrionics of Carnici and Ciafardini. He had a surprise witness. A local photographer, Thomas Withrow, testified that he had been approached by Charles Lester on April 14, well prior to the incident of May 9, about taking a picture of a man and woman at some later date. He was promised that he would be well paid for the picture. Withrow initially agreed and was sent by Lester to see a man named Marty at the Glen Hotel. Marty told Withrow that "they'll be in a room. We'll open the door, you take the picture, and we'll jump out." Withrow, after leaving the meeting, decided that he didn't want any part of the scheme and decided not to do it. He told his wife that if a man named Marty called for him, she should "tell him I'm not here!" The photographer's story was corroborated by his grandmother and wife, who testified that she had received several frantic calls from the Tropicana looking for the photographer on the night of the May 9 incident. Newport Special Counsel Thomas Hirschfiled, stunned by the obvious implication of a frame-up, approached the police court judge, stating that he believed the witnesses and thought that the case should be investigated by the grand jury. The prosecutor said he would never have brought the charges if he had this information. The judge agreed and dismissed the case against George Ratterman. More importantly, the national press coverage of the trial impelled the governor to act on the affidavits he had previously received.

The governor ordered an investigation and initiated removal proceedings against elected officials in Campbell County and Newport. Governor Combs ultimately charged Sheriff Roll, Newport Police Chief Gugel, Newport Detective Chief Fredericks and Campbell County Police Chief Stuart with neglect of duty. Gugel and Fredericks resigned from office before the hearings were held, but the hearings proceeded. Both were found guilty of neglect of duty and prohibited from holding public office for four years. Sheriff Roll and County Police Chief Stuart were ousted, but they were later pardoned by the governor once the heat died down.

During the hearings into the governor's removal petition, a Newport madam named Hattie Jackson testified that she had made weekly payoffs to Commonwealth Attorney Wise, Judge Murphy, Chief Gugel, Detective Ciafardini and individual officers on the police force. A special Campbell County grand jury was convened, and indictments were finally issued. Ironically, Judge Murphy was prevented from overseeing the grand jury. Judge Edward Hill, the tamer of Bloody Harlan, took his place. Judge

Hill removed Commonwealth Attorney Wise when he became a subject of investigation. The grand jury returned ninety-three felony accounts in nineteen indictments for setting up and operating gambling houses. Also indicted on charges of conspiracy to pervert justice were Newport's Mayor Mussman and City Manager Hesch, now ex-chief of police Gugel, now ex-detective Chief Fredericks, Detectives Ciafardini, Upshire White, Edward Gugel (son of ex-chief Gugel), three other police officers and three city commissioners. Commonwealth Attorney Wise was not indicted, but he was publicly chastised for his apathetic attitude toward gambling and prostitution in the county.

Frank Benton, the commonwealth attorney "pro tem" appointed by the governor to replace William Wise, stated that "the Grand Jury that I advised didn't indict Bill Wise and Ray Murphy, but we knew they were corrupt and paid by the mob." In 1963, Benton would defeat Wise for commonwealth attorney. Judge Ray Murphy was also defeated in the same election. Benton also stated that he received a phone call offering him $4,000 a week if he would leave the syndicate alone. One has to view this phone call with some skepticism. Offering the large sum of $4,000 a week would require the assets of either the Cleveland Four or Meyer Lansky, but it is extremely unlikely that they would make a bribe offer over the phone. Nevertheless, the trial of those indicted would take a typical Newport twist in 1963.

The INS began investigating to see if any prostitutes had been imported into Newport. The IRS checked the known gambling spots to see if they were displaying the required gambling stamps. In 1959, 1 out of every 145 adult residents of Newport had a fifty-dollar gambling stamp. The sheriff's election was still months away, and the federal government was in the process of getting involved, but things were going to get complicated.

On May 26, ten days after the charges against Ratterman were dismissed, the Campbell County grand jury indicted Tito Cainci and Tom Paisley of conspiring to have Ratterman arrested. The truth about Paisley's involvement will probably never be known; however, later events and statements by April Flowers strongly suggest that Ratterman's confidence in his "friend" was misplaced. On June 20, the two went to trial with Judge Ray L. Murphy presiding. Commonwealth Attorney William Wise, in what could be called a halfhearted attempt to prosecute the case, called only two witnesses, George Ratterman and Cincinnati pathologist Dr. Frank Cleveland, before resting the state's case on the second day. Ratterman testified that it was absurd to believe that Paisley had anything to do with it. Paisley's lawyer asked that the charge be dismissed. Judge Murphy ordered the jury to return a not-guilty verdict because there was "not an iota of proof or evidence to show that the two men set up Mr. Ratterman as he testified." In another bizarre twist to an already bizarre set of events, Judge Murphy would later file a motion in Campbell County Circuit Court to have Ratterman permanently disbarred as an attorney. Ratterman was given a temporary writ of prohibition against this being tried in the Campbell County Circuit Court, and the Court of Appeals of Kentucky granted a permanent prohibition.

Even though the charges against Paisley and Carinci had been dismissed at the local level, cleanup efforts were beginning outside of the local jurisdiction and control. Governor Combs declared a state of emergency and sent state police in to enforce the law. On August 22, 1961, special agents of the Intelligence Division of the Internal Revenue Service raided Screw Andrew's Sportsman's Club and shut it down. The voluminous evidence gathered during their raid would be used in a special federal grand jury to be convened in Covington.

In the later part of August, Senator John McClellan was holding Congressional hearings on organized crime. The *Courier-Journal* reported that the committee subpoenaed three Kentucky witnesses: Richard Busker and Stanley Schomaker, co-owners of the Belmont Snax in Newport; and Louis Efkeman, publisher of the *Louisville Daily Sports News*. Busker and Schroeder reportedly handled $1,165,000 in betting wagers in a twenty-one-day period in May. Efkeman was said to have bought three million betting slips for later sale to bookmakers from 1959 to 1961. It was also alleged that Thomas Kelly, a former member of the Capone Syndicate, had a third interest in the *Louisville Daily Sports News*. The three gamblers asserted their Fifth Amendment rights seventy-nine times before the committee, even after being threatened with contempt. Senator McClellan had Efkeman's second-class mailing permit removed. Even though local reform groups were relying on the hope that the election of George Ratterman would ensure the cleanup of Campbell County and Newport, the federal government was to play a huge role, if not the dominant one, in the cleanup of Kentucky's Sin City.

Part Five

THE CLEANUP BEGINS IN KENTUCKY'S SIN CITY

FEDERAL INTERVENTION

Ronald Goldfarb provides the best description of federal action against the criminal elements in Northern Kentucky and the trial of those accused of violating George Ratterman's civil rights. Sent to Kentucky the day after Ratterman's arrest with the title of special assistant to the attorney general, Goldfarb had the authority to conduct grand jury investigations into potential federal crimes in Kentucky. He ended up with two federal grand juries operating in Lexington and Covington, Kentucky, and one in Cincinnati, Ohio. The one in Lexington was investigating the possible civil rights violations. The Covington grand jury was investigating Newport violations, and the Cincinnati grand jury was investigating the illegal numbers operation in the Cincinnati-Newport region, particularly the Sportsman Club run by Screw Andrews.

CIVIL RIGHTS VIOLATIONS—LEXINGTON GRAND JURY

At first, Robert Kennedy decided that the federal government would not take action until after the sheriff's election so as not to be accused of interfering in local politics, but the local reformers insisted on federal intervention as soon as possible. However, the largely circumstantial case was not going to be easy. The investigation into the possible civil rights violations surrounding the arrest and "frame-up" of sheriff's candidate George Ratterman would present problems. First, the Civil Rights Act, under which they would seek indictments, arising out of the Civil War Reconstruction statutes, dealt with civil rights violations defined as depriving another person of any right protected by the United States Constitution by public officials acting under the color of law. Under "color of law" means that the person doing the act is using powers that have been given to them by a governmental agency. False arrest and fabrication of evidence by public officials, such as the Newport police officers Ciafardini, Quitter and White, would certainly be included under a civil rights violation committed under color of law. There was reason to be believe that Ciafardini had acted in conspiracy with Lester, Carinci and Buckler to frame Ratterman. However, even though there was reason to believe that Quitter and White were corrupt police officers, there was no evidence, other than the fact that they were there when the arrest was made, that they were involved in the conspiracy. That left Ciafardini as the most likely public official to target.

The next set of problems, and possibly the most damaging, was presented by George Ratterman himself. Ratterman and his "friend" Paisley could remember little of the night's events, supposedly as a result of being slipped the "Mickey Finns." However, there was no evidence that chloral hydrate had been given to Paisley, and there was dispute over when it had been given to Ratterman. Lester and his cabal claimed Ratterman took it after he was released from jail, thus providing a justification for his actions. Further complicating the events was the fact that the evening had featured a drinking binge by the reformer and his friend—maybe not the first. According to Goldberg, Ratterman had consumed eleven scotch and waters, certainly enough, by themselves, to create confusion and a lack of memory. Goldberg and his team had to be sure that Ratterman was telling the truth before seeking indictments.

Ratterman volunteered to take a lie detector examination to demonstrate that he was telling the truth. The exam was given, but the results were inconclusive. The examiner was unable to say if Ratterman was being deceptive or not. Goldberg said that Ratterman was a bad subject for the lie detector because he had a genius IQ and talked too much. Ratterman gave lengthy answers to the questions posed by the examiner. A second exam was given, with Ratterman instructed to give yes-no answers. The second exam found no evidence of deception. Based on these results, their knowledge of corruption and organized crime in Newport and the circumstantial evidence of a frame-up, the federal team decided to continue the grand jury investigation into possible civil rights violations. But they were still not ready to seek indictments without further conclusive evidence. This frustrated the Lexington grand jury, even leading to calls from the foreman to Robert Kennedy complaining about the overly hesitant actions of Goldberg and his team. The members of the grand jury wanted action taken before the November 7 election, fearing that inaction would lead to Ratterman's defeat and the end of the reform effort. An unexpected witness made the case and speeded up the process.

April Flowers, supposedly under pangs of conscience, called a Cincinnati television reporter and told him she had important information about the Ratterman case but she would only talk to FBI Agent Frank Staab. Agent Staab was on the team Goldberg had put together. Arrangements were made to interview Flowers in Covington, Kentucky. For four hours, Goldberg, Staab and Bill Lynch, another attorney with the Justice Department, listened to her rendition of what happened. First, she was given a lie detector exam, which she passed with flying colors. Her testimony led the team to the following theory of what happened.

Ratterman was having a drink with Tom Paisley at a hotel in Cincinnati. Tito Carinci had previously arranged with Paisley to "bump" into them because he wanted to talk with Ratterman. At the bar, Carinci surreptitiously poured chloral hydrate into Ratterman's drink. Ratterman began feeling the effects, and Paisley offered to drive him home. On the way home, Ratterman passed out. Carinci, and possibly Marty Bucceri, dragged Ratterman to Carinci's room at the Tropicana and put him in bed with April. Paisley was waylaid by Rita Desmond, another stripper at the club. When the previously arranged photographer could not be found, the police were called and Ratterman was arrested. This prosecutor's theory does not exactly fit the muddled statement by Ratterman and suggests that Paisley was more involved than he admitted; however, it supported the argument that Ratterman's civil rights were violated under color of law. Lester, Carinci and Buckler had conspired with a public official, Newport Detective Ciafardini, or possibly all three detectives, to frame Ratterman, therefore depriving him of his civil rights.

JUANITA HODGES (A.K.A. APRIL FLOWERS) STATEMENT

Rita Desmond and a man I now know to be Thomas Paisley were in Carinci's living room. They told me to go into the bedroom and I did. I saw a man on the bed I have never seen before. He was fully clothed and unconscious. I did not know who the man on the bed was, but I have since learned it was George Ratterman, candidate for sheriff of Campbell County, Kentucky. Other employees at the club have since told me Carinci and Paisley almost carried Ratterman into the club. When I went into the room, I room, I said "Hey, wake up." He didn't respond, so I went back to the living room. Rita and Paisley had left so I mixed a drink and went back into the bedroom.

With this theory of what happened, Goldfarb and Lynch returned to Washington to discuss the bill of indictment. It was signed by all their bosses, including Attorney General Robert Kennedy. The Lexington federal grand jury was called back into session on October 26, 1961, just days before the November 7 election. April Flowers and Rita Desmond (she had heard Charles Lester tell April to lie), appeared before the grand jury. April Flowers said that she had been promised a trip to Puerto Rico if she cooperated, but the orchestrators of the Gangland Gong Show had reneged on their promise. By 4:10 p.m., the grand jury said there was evidence that Charles Lester, Tito Carinci, Marty Bucceri and Detectives Ciafardini, Quitter and White had conspired to violate Ratterman's civil rights. The policemen had acted under color of law. They had used their police powers to deprive George Ratterman of his constitutional rights.

The indictments were announced by Attorney General Robert Kennedy in Washington. The grand jury also released a blistering report saying that testimony revealed that elected and appointed officials were receiving payoffs for non-enforcement of the law, that there had been no effort on the part of the commonwealth, county or city attorneys to carry out their sworn duties and that there had been no effort on the part of local police or the sheriff's department to enforce the laws against gambling and vice. The blistering report and the indictments created another media frenzy that could only help Ratterman's campaign.

THE ELECTION

Several months before the election, members of the Cleveland Syndicate were trying to portray themselves as "good guys" also interested in chasing the "bad guys" out of Newport. Specifically, their goal was to portray a "syndicate image" patterned along "Big Brother" lines. Their campaign had two main points. First, the syndicate wanted a "clean" Newport, but it was opposed to reformers who wanted a "closed" Newport.

The idea that "honest" gambling is all right, but bust-out joints and prostitution are bad for business was certainly an idea that had appeal for local businessmen. "Clean up, not close up" had worked before; it might work again. However, it had two basic flaws. Earlier reform efforts based on "clean up, not close up" had accomplished neither. The sheriff's election might not be determined by the votes coming from Newport, where the gamblers and vice operators had always been able to "turn out the vote" by any means possible. The reform effort had grown up in the suburban cities like Fort Thomas. There just might be a change in the power structure in Campbell County.

The second point the syndicate emphasized was that the syndicate did not frame George Ratterman because Ratterman "hasn't a chance" to win his race for sheriff. This was probably true and made a lot of sense. No one would have suspected that organized crime figures would have engaged in farce conducted at the Tropicana. As Robert Kennedy often said, organized crime members may be criminals and murderers, but they are good businessmen. What happened at the Tropicana was bad for business. However, the basic flaw with this argument is that the conspirators that put together the frame-up had felt safe in doing so because they knew that the police, the commonwealth attorney, the judges and the rest of the political structure were under their control or subject to their influence. The reason for this was the result of the gambling and vice in the city and county, whether it was syndicate or independent controlled.

Newport was dark and deserted the day before the election. The casinos were padlocked. Unemployed pimps, gamblers and prostitutes—that is, those who had not already left for Las Vegas or the Bahamas—waited for the results. Messick reported that, even before the election, every plane leaving Kentucky for Las Vegas had been crowded with gamblers hoping to find work. Did they think the election was a forgone conclusion, or had they recognized what the Cleveland Syndicate and other organized crime figures already knew: the future was in Nevada, where gambling was legal. Some of the remaining independent bosses plotted their time-honored strategy of ghost voters and repeat voters. The Switch to Honesty Party representing George Ratterman and the other reform candidates had poll watchers ready to challenge unqualified voters and keep the election honest.

On election day, the Switch to Honesty Party poll watchers were kept busy. In one precinct, a large number of women who had worked in brothels were successfully challenged. This particular precinct had 144 registered voters with only 44 qualified. Automobiles with large American flags and green "Local Self Government" stickers were seen throughout "Sin City," carrying voters from one precinct to another as they were denied their right to vote more than once. Someone threw a brick through the plate-glass window of Ratterman's headquarters. The workers seized on the vandalism by decorating the hole with red, white and blue ribbons.

As darkness fell on that cold November day, a mood of optimism began to grow at Ratterman's headquarters as unofficial results were phoned in from the courthouse by Ratterman's poll watchers. Even though Ratterman was not given much of a chance by the Kentucky political pundits, the supporters sensed victory. At 9:00 p.m., the results were in. There were more than 26,000 votes cast, an off-year election record. Ratterman carried Campbell with 12,600 votes. Attorney Lester's main man, Johnny "TV" Peluso, the operator of a television repair store and the Democratic nominee, received 7,070 votes. Ratterman did lose the popular vote in Newport to Peluso by 500 votes. The small vote margin in Newport was considered a major victory for the reform candidate. The only bad news in the election was that the four reform candidates for the Newport city commission were all narrowly defeated. However, the election of Ratterman, a reform candidate from the suburb of Fort Thomas, signaled that reform was on its way and the power in Campbell County had shifted from Sin City to the suburbs, where it remains even today.

AFTER THE ELECTION

Governor Bert Combs, pleased by the election results, renewed his pledge to "stamp out commercialized vice in Newport as long as I am governor." The head of the Alcoholic Beverage Control Board went to Newport and personally pulled the liquor licenses of the casinos for gambling infractions. In an unusual move, the state transportation department issued a regulation making it illegal for common carriers, including taxis and trucks, to make stops with passengers or goods at locations where illegal gambling took place. Combined with this move, the Public Service Commission issued a regulation to allow telephone companies to disconnect phones from any structure used for gambling or other illegal actions. The clubs and casinos shut down and waited for the storm to blow over as it always had; however, the layoff betting operations shut down and moved to Terre Haute, Indiana, another city with Cleveland Syndicate connections. Illegal off-track and sports betting reportedly disappeared overnight. The IRS reported a 20 percent decline in the countrywide volume of legal wagers reported from 1961 to 1962, and there was a $200,000 decline in illegal bets reported by the Justice Department. Attorney General Robert Kennedy stated that 40 percent of the decline was due to the cleanup in Newport. In 1962, a mysterious fire consumed the Tropicana Club, the scene of Ratterman's frame-up.

In 1962, a combined effort on the part of sheriff's deputies led by George Ratterman and IRS agents closed the gambling joints in Newport. The deputies raided all the joints having federal wagering tax stamps, and the federal agents raided those not having tax stamps. In early 1963, Ratterman would announce that illegal gambling "has practically been eliminated from Campbell County." It was getting hot for gamblers and vice operators in Newport and Campbell County. Organized crime's influence was ending, although it was not entirely gone. But vice and "disorganized" gambling by homegrown citizens not connected to the syndicate would remain in Newport for at least the next twenty years. Sin City was not to give up its "sin" easily. The Newport twist to criminal prosecutions would appear again.

FEDERAL ACTION

The federal government was also moving on its own soon after the election. In December, ex–Campbell County Sheriff Roll was indicted by a federal grand jury on four counts of failing to file income tax months. In the same month, another federal grand jury indicted Screw Andrews, his brother Spider, two of his nephews and four others on thirty-five counts of wagering tax evasion.

The conspiracy trial for violating George Ratterman's civil rights, *U.S. v. Lester et al.*, began on June 5, 1962, in the federal courthouse in Covington, Kentucky, across the Licking River from Newport.

The trial opened with a crowded courtroom and numerous media representatives present. U.S. Attorneys Ronald Goldfarb and Bill Lynch represented the federal government, and four well-known and experienced trial lawyers represented the defendants, Carinci, Bucceri, Lester, Detective Ciafardini and Officers Quitter and White. Goldfarb read the indictments and highlighted the evidence to be produced. Tom Steuve, the attorney for Carinci and Bucceri, told the court that Ratterman had sought out Carinci on the night in question and returned to the Glenn Hotel (Tropicana), despite Carinci's protests. Lester's lawyer, Leonard White, said that Lester had done no more than be a good lawyer acting for his clients. The lawyers for the police officers stressed that they had not been part of any conspiracy and had only performed their duties as policemen on the night in question. Ratterman was not drugged, and he had been treated fairly; after all, he had been acquitted of the charges involved. It was now time for the prosecution to put on its case.

George Ratteman was the first witness. He presented all the details he could remember and then withstood two days of contentious cross-examination by the four defense attorneys. Henry Cook, Ratterman's lawyer and the lawyer for the Committee of 500, went up next and filled in the missing parts of Ratterman's testimony—what happened after the arrest. Now that they had testimony that Ratterman was innocent, Goldfarb and Lynch went on the offensive, showing who was guilty.

The officers who had gone with Detective Ciafardini to the FOP meeting in Bowling Green the day before the incident were put on the stand. They testified that Ciafardini had asked them to lie to cover up some awkward facts. Tom Winthow, the commercial photographer who had been approached by Lester to take the picture, his wife and grandmother all testified next. After all, it was their testimony that had resulted in the dismissal of the charges against Ratterman in the Newport trail.

Following adjournment for the weekend, Juanita Hodges (a.k.a. April Flowers) took the stand. She was the star and the most notorious of the government's witnesses, as well as the most anticipated. She began by explaining why she had come forward and recanted her earlier testimony. Her mother was dying of cancer and she felt terrible about her life and wanted to do something honorable. Flowers added that she felt bad for Ratterman and couldn't live with herself for what she had done.

She recounted how Carinci had hustled her up to his room, where she found Tom Paisley and Rita Desmond sitting on the couch. She went into the bedroom, where she found a fully clothed George Ratterman in a stupor, grunting and blinking. She went back to the outer room, but Paisley and Rita had left for Rita's room. Within minutes, the three policemen rushed in. She knew Ciafardini because he dated one of the waitresses and had visited the waitress earlier. When she asked Ciafardini what was going on, he winked at her, indicating it was a phony arrest. She then said that she heard a commotion in the next room, and Ratterman was brought out with his pants off, wrapped in a bedspread.

The last part of her testimony implicated Attorney Charles Lester in the conspiracy. Flowers said that she made two trips to Lester's office with Carinci and Bucceri. On both occasions, Lester told her to just listen to what Carinci and the police said, agree with them and make her story as dirty as possible. She went along with them because "I was told to keep my mouth shut and nothing would happen. They'd say things like: people who talk wind up in the river. I was scared."

At this time, the federal prosecutors, sensing that the powerful testimony of April Flowers and George Ratterman had made their case, decided not to call the weak and nervous Tom Paisley to the stand. They were afraid that he would hurt their case. His actions that night were still under a cloud of suspicion. The bottom line was that Tom Paisley was not a credible witness. Mrs. Ratterman testified about the events of May 8 and 9, and then the medical experts testified about the presence of chloral hydrate in Ratterman's system. The last person to testify was the FBI agent Frank Staab, who had interviewed over five hundred persons in connection with his year-long investigation. His testimony was compelling. The prosecution rested. They had laid out a powerful case revealing the conspiracy to violate the civil rights of George Ratterman, or so they thought.

The defense put on each of the defendants, who denied any wrongdoing. The usual legal maneuvering commenced with the defendants asking for a directed verdict of acquittal, all of which were promptly denied by the judge. The summations lasted a full day, and the case was turned over to the jury for deliberation. The national news media waited for a verdict, Washington and Attorney General Kennedy waited for a verdict and the U.S. Attorneys Goldfarb and Lynch waited for a verdict. After several days of deliberation, the jury informed the judge that they were hopelessly deadlocked. The judge refused the defendants request for a mistrial after the prosecutors told him they were prepared to retry the case as soon as it was feasible. However, the shocked U.S. attorneys were not sure if Washington would give the go-ahead for a new trial. The verdict was another bizarre twist to events in Kentucky's Sin City.

The prosecutors licked their wounds and started getting ready for the trial of Frank "Screw" Andrews and the seven other numbers operators. The case was tried in the same Covington courtroom with the same federal judge. The trial lasted a month as the IRS analyzed reams of documents confiscated in the raid of the Sportsman Club a year earlier. None of the defendants testified in this trial, fearing cross-examination about their criminal exploits and the possibility of perjury if they lied. After several days of deliberation, which had Goldfarb and Lynch fearful of another hung jury, the jury found all defendants guilty. The judge sentenced most to five years in prison and Screw Andrews to six years. This case shut down the numbers operation in Newport and Cincinnati. The combined efforts of the federal, state and local authorities were bringing reform. However, there was more to be done. Commonwealth Attorney William Wise and Judge Ray Murphy were still in office, the Newport public officials indicted by the Campbell County grand jury had not been tried, Attorney Charles Lester and the other conspirators were free and remnants of the syndicate and independent bust-out joints remained in Newport. And there were still many in Newport—public officials, businessmen and citizens—who thought the city should remain Cincinnati's playground, even if that meant wide-open sleaze and not wide-open gambling. They were apparently comfortable with Newport's reputation as Kentucky's Sin City.

Part Six

SIN CITY NO MORE?

GAMBLING

As far as gambling and organized crime were concerned, Newport's reign as America's Sin City was over, thanks in large part to federal actions. Even before the first trial of the Ratterman conspirators, the federal government had taken action. In 1961, Attorney General Robert Kennedy convinced Congress to pass legislation that ended Newport's reign as the largest layoff betting center east of Las Vegas. The three anticrime bills passed by Congress made it illegal to engage in interstate travel for illegal purposes, to engage in interstate transportation of gambling materials and to engage in interstate transmission of bets and racing information. Probably the most important part of the legislation allowed for court-approved wiretaps to gather incriminating evidence. The nature of illegal betting information, instantaneous transmission of bets and racing information through phone lines made them easily discoverable through wiretaps. A major wire service in New Orleans that serviced betting operations in Mississippi; Hot Springs, Arkansas; and Newport, Kentucky, went out of business. Newport's Gil Beckley was indicted in this New Orleans case for running a layoff betting operation out of the Glenn Hotel, the hotel where Ratterman was framed.

Illegal off-track and sports betting disappeared overnight. The Justice Department estimated that illegal betting fell by one-fifth of a billion dollars from 1961 to 1962. Attorney General Kennedy attributed 40 percent of that drop to the cleanup of Newport. News sources reported that the number of handbook licenses issued for use in Newport dropped from 149 in 1961 to two in 1962. Justice Department actions against Screw Andrews shut down the numbers racket in Newport and Cincinnati. The state and local authorities, led by the newly elected sheriff, were also making moves on the casinos and bust-out joints. By 1963, Ratterman asserted that "illegal gambling has practically been eliminated from Campbell County." And it had. But the gamblers did not give up.

Screw Andrews got out of prison in 1965 and promptly reopened the Sportsman's Club. After the gambling indictments of the early 1960s, many of the casinos had reopened as illegal bingo halls, under the leadership of Red Masterson, and were continuing limited illegal gambling operations. Screw joined them. But in 1968, federal marshals raided the bingo halls and shut them down.

The cessation of illegal gambling was not without its costs to Newport. *Newport, Kentucky: A Bicentennial History* reports that the city's treasury lost $100,000 in payroll taxes and licensing fees in 1961. The central retail district declined. Visitors to the clubs and bust-out joints had spent freely at the restaurants, liquor stores and local merchant shops that had stayed open in the late evenings and early mornings. The *Bicentennial History* gives the example of Ebert's Meats, located at 939 Monmouth Street in the heart of the gambling district, as an illustration of the impact on local merchants. Ebert's opened at 4:00 a.m. on Saturdays, and by 6:00 a.m. it would make more money than it would the rest of the day by selling steaks to lucky gamblers. The loss to the city treasury and business interests was overlooked by later city politicians. After all, gambling and organized crime was tolerated and condoned for over a century, and reform efforts had come and gone during that time. Newport was still Newport, and gambling was not the only vice in Newport.

TRIALS AND RETRIALS

Attorney General Kennedy approved the retrial of the Ratterman case, and Ronald Goldfarb planned the government's strategy. Although it would be risky to put Paisley on the stand because of the allegations that Tom Paisley "whored around and engaged in drinking binges with George Ratterman," this time Paisley would testify. All the prosecutors could do is hope that Ratterman and Paisley "boozing all night" and Paisley running around with a showgirl wouldn't hurt their case. Goldfarb writes, "Putting on Paisley as our witness is going to be as much fun as having root canal work. But there's no alternative." Not putting him on the stand had damaged the prosecution's case in the first trial. Defense attorneys had raised the issue of why the government had not put on a friendly witness, creating doubt in the jurors' minds. It was also decided to attack attorney Charles Lester's argument that he was a reputable lawyer. He was the main target of the prosecutors because it was evident that Lester was the "brains" behind the conspiracy. The prosecutors had by now learned of his earlier disbarment and his bad reputation for veracity among his colleagues in the legal community. They also learned that Lester had been indicted for attempted rape and pleaded guilty to assault and battery.

The second trial started at 10:00 a.m. on July 15, 1963, with the same judge. With the exception of Tom Paisley, the same prosecution witnesses testified. Rita Desmond, now married with the new name of Bonnie Noe, testified that Paisley was a drunken girl chaser. As expected, Charles Lester took the stand, and the prosecution was ready. It was brought out that Lester had been reprimanded on several charges by the Kentucky Court of Appeals. Mitch Miller, former assistant U.S. attorney in Lexington and now counsel to the Kentucky State Bar Association, was called to the stand as a character witness to testify about Lester's reputation for veracity in the legal community. He testified that Lester's reputation for truth and veracity was highly questionable. With this bullet to Lester's heart, the prosecution rested.

The government presented what it thought to be a powerful case against the Ratterman conspirators. But that's what it thought it had done in the first trial, which had ended with a hung jury. The prosecutors also knew that if there were no verdicts this time, there would not be a third trial. So they waited for the jury to decide. The jury took three days to arrive at a decision, and it was an odd one. Charles Lester and Buccieri were found guilty of conspiracy, and Carinici and the three police officers, Ciafardini, Quitter and White, were all acquitted. The judge sentenced Lester and Buccieri to the maximum twelve months in prison. They appealed and lost. Buccieri decided against further appeals and served his sentence. Lester, facing disbarment, appealed further. Lester's appeal to the United States Supreme Court was denied, and he served his sentence and was disbarred. In 1974, Lester applied for reinstatement. The Court of Appeals of Kentucky turned down his application.

In 1965, Tito Carinci was convicted of tax evasion and sentenced to three years in prison. He did not return to Newport after serving out his sentence. Carinci was also convicted in 1981 of dealing in heroin and served five years of a twenty-year sentence. The three policemen went back to work and eventually retired from the Newport Police Department. Ciafardini retired in 1972 with the rank of head of detectives. In a 2002 *Kentucky Post* article, the eighty-five-year-old Ciafardini was quoted as saying, "George Ratterman was not set up. I will go to my grave saying so. Ratterman was looking for (sex). But how are you gonna beat the Kennedays once they get mixed up in it." Upshire White changed his first name to Upshere and was the chief of police from 1961 to 1967. George Ratterman ran unsuccessfully for congressman in 1966 and shortly thereafter moved to Colorado, where he died in 2007.

SLEAZE CITY—THE STRIP OF GREATER CINCINNATI

In the 1970s, the gamblers had moved to Las Vegas. Their places were taken by independents, who moved into vice in the form of strip shows, peep shows, prostitution and some video poker machines. Organized crime had been replaced by disorganized vice operators willing to take advantage of the political situation and social conditions still existing in Newport: a consumer market, a community in need of profit-making businesses and corruption. These very same conditions created the climate for organized crime's long stay in Sin City. A 1980 *Kentucky Post* article provides the following description of Monmouth Street in Newport:

> *Today, Monmouth Street is lined with deserted store fronts, junk shops, chili parlors and seven go-go bars. Peep shows and strip joints have replaced the plush casinos. Monmouth Street gives Newport the look of a city in decline.*

"Big Jim" Harris, the former marshal of Wilder who ran the prostitution racket at the Hi-De-Ho Club in the 1950s, was operating the Jai-Alai Piano Lounge (there was no piano) on York Street. The sixty-five-year-old Harris was convicted of promoting lewdness (prostitution) at the Jai-Alai Club in 1973. He was fined $5,000 and given two years in prison. Even though Harris was a twice-convicted felon, the *Cincinnati Post* reported that he was a member of Newport's Fraternal Order of Police and had just paid for a celebration party for Newport's new chief of police. The other clubs on Monmouth and York Street, with names like the Brass Mule Lounge, the Body Shoppe, the Mouse Trap, Talk of the Town, the Pink Panther, Dillenger's Lounge and the Delta Street Lounge, featured exotic dancers with names like Trixie Delight,

Amber Snow and Liberty Belle. La Madame's was a topless bar. In addition to the exotic dancers, there were plenty of bar girls hustling out-of-towners and visitors from Cincinnati for drinks. There was even a topless billiard parlor. The clubs were often no more than a large room with a bar, some tables and a stripper's runway. Some of the peep shows, where customers shuffled from one booth to the other feeding quarters to the projectors, were making up to $4,000 weekly. Cinema X was charging $6 admission to see skin flicks and X-rated movies.

A 1980 story in *Enquirer* magazine described the experiences of an undercover reporter who worked as a bar girl in the Brass Ass strip joint for a week. The bar girls' customers were primarily out-of-town visitors and businessmen attending conventions in Cincinnati. The girls, over a dozen in this one place, received receipts for every drink the men bought them. At the end of the night, the girls cashed in the receipts for money. The reporter made forty-six dollars the first night. The drinks served to the girls at four to eight dollars apiece were mostly soda pop and a sprinkling of liquor. The "mixers," or sales representatives as the girls were known, seldom drank the drinks bought for them, pouring them out under the table or some other convenient place. The mixer's job was to get rid of the drink as soon as possible and persuade the man to buy another one.

CLEANUP AGAIN

In September 1981, a story under the banner "Newport's bright lights are going dim" appeared in the *Kentucky Post*. The adult entertainment joints on York and Monmouth Streets were reeling from a series of raids by the state police and actions by the liquor control boards. "Big Jim" Harris, the former marshal of Wilder and owner of the Jai-Alai Piano Lounge, had pleaded guilty to promoting prostitution in circuit court. As this was at least his third conviction of prostitution-related charges, he was enjoined from owning or participating in the business by the state Board of Alcoholic Beverage Control. The Mouse Trap lost its liquor license following a state police raid that resulted in the owner and manager being charged with promoting prostitution. The Body Shoppe, Delta Street Lounge, Dillenger's and the Pink Panther faced action by the ABC board following drug and prostitution raids by the state police. The Pink Panther and Dillenger's faced additional action by the city for zoning violations. A Newport zoning ordinance said that adult-entertainment businesses could not be located within two hundred feet of a church or school. Dillenger's closed, waiting for the outcome.

Several other joints, seeing the handwriting on the wall, were trying to sell their liquor licenses. At least two adult bookstores closed under pressure from prosecutors on obscenity charges. The Cinema X Theater was raided seven times in twelve months by state police, resulting in four convictions and a $222,000 fine. The Brass Mule and the Talk of the Town Lounge were the only remaining clubs offering nude dancing.

Newport's bright lights may have been growing dim, but they were not extinguished. That would take another ten years. The wide-open nature of sleaze clubs brought with them a question: how could they have operated so wide open in the 1970s? The answer could be found in the recurring nature of scandal and reform in Newport's history for over a hundred years—political corruption. *Newport, Kentucky: A Bicentennial History* reports that citizen groups had been suspecting political corruption for some time. Citizens wondered if their municipal government was operating honestly and efficiently. Internal Revenue agents routinely targeted municipal leaders for scrutiny. It was becoming common knowledge that public officials were accepting kickbacks from contractors. The city commissioners were holding closed-door meetings in violation of the state's open-meeting law. Police officers were frequenting the strip clubs off duty and were moonlighting in the clubs as bouncers. They were openly associating with convicted felons, such as Big Jim Harris. In the early 1980s, the suspicions were confirmed.

In the 1980s, a former mayor served six years in federal prison for perjury and conspiracy to commit extortion, a public works director received a two-year sentence for extortion and several contractors were found guilty of bribery. The police department was rocked by scandal and corruption. A police chief was indicted on six counts of forgery and theft. A reform chief, David Williams, took over the Newport Police Department in 1982 and promptly fired a third of his forty-five-member department. A new reform effort was set to begin.

THE LAST (MOST RECENT) REFORM EFFORT

Whether or not the most recent reform effort in Newport is the last in the cycle of scandal-reform-scandal-reform in Newport's history remains to be seen. The existence of gambling and organized crime's involvement in

Newport up until the 1960s relied on the same set of circumstances that allowed for the existence of vice operations after the gamblers moved on.

Since at least the 1950s, the political climate in Newport has been described as the battle between two groups, the Liberals and the Reformers. The Liberals practiced the old-style patronage politics in which favors translated into votes and "honest graft"—a system popular in other cities with histories of organized crime. The Liberals had a laissez faire attitude toward gambling and the adult-entertainment businesses as long as they improved the local economy and city treasury. Not all were corrupt, but those who weren't turned what was known as the "Newport Eye" toward gambling and, now, sleaze. They may not have endorsed the gambling and sleaze, but they condoned it, or at least remained neutral. The Reformers, on the other hand, were opposed to the gambling and the sleaze and wanted all of it stopped.

Irene Deaton, a Newport housewife with eight children, is considered to be the most notable early leader of the latest reform effort. After an unsuccessful run, she was elected to the commission in 1975. The reformers took control of the city commission in 1977, when other reformers were elected. Mrs. Deaton was elected mayor in 1980, but the Liberals regained control of the city commission in the same election. However, by 1980, the public was becoming discontented with the Liberal city commission. The final straw came when the city commission voted to repeal a city ordinance limiting the number of bars that could stay open to 3:00 a.m. in residential neighborhoods. The commission meetings became such a verbal free-for-all that the Liberals posted police guards at public meetings and ejected critics.

The heavy-handed actions of the city commission jumpstarted the reform organizations into action. The Newport Political Action Committee (NEWPAC) formed, endorsed and helped finance a campaign—a reform ticket. This group, reminiscent of the Committee of 500 and their support of George Ratterman, urged the complete replacement of the city commission. In 1981, four NEWPAC-endorsed candidates won, and by the elections of 1983, all of the Liberals were gone.

The NEWPAC commissioners were able to pass an ordinance in 1982 that outlawed nudity in establishments that sold alcohol. They were also able to pass strict zoning ordinances that prevented the spread of adult-entertainment clubs. The police department, under the leadership of the newly appointed Chief Williams, increased its surveillance over bars, making numerous vice arrests.

Newport's anti-obscenity ordinance was appealed all the way to the U.S. Supreme Court, where it was upheld in 1986. Seven of the sixteen exotic-dancing operating in 1982 had their liquor licenses temporarily suspended by 1986. In 1991, there were twelve exotic-dancing clubs left, and they were under constant pressure from the police. Two of the clubs surrendered their liquor licenses in an attempt to avoid the new ordinance. Technically, they avoided prosecution, but they lost money. In 1996, there were six exotic-dancing clubs left. That number was cut to three in 1999 and two in 2003.

CONCLUSION

The history of gambling, prostitution and organized crime in Newport, Kentucky, is not appreciably different from similar histories of the dozen or so other open cities of the 1940s and 1950s. For that matter, it is not very different from the history of organized crime in the largest American cities, like New York, Chicago, Atlantic City, Philadelphia or Boston. It is that lack of difference that makes this a compelling story. Whether in a small river town in Kentucky or a metropolis like New York, organized crime operates in much the same way in very different places and under very different circumstances. The mystery of organized crime's persistence and success is really no mystery at all. It revolves around some very basic truths: organized crime, politics, the economy and American society, all of which are confirmed by events in Newport.

Organized crime is first and foremost a profit-making enterprise, a business. As such, it must conform to the exigencies of the market in which it operates, both in terms of how it organizes itself and how it serves its customers. Newport is a classic case of crime as a business. Even the largest syndicates operating in Newport segmented their operations by using local managers and keeping syndicate "leaders" away from the actual delivery of illicit goods and services. Moe Dalitz was in Las Vegas, Morris Kleinman was in Cleveland and then Miami, Louis Rothkopf was in Miami and Sam Tucker moved to Florida in the late 1940s. Ed Levinson left early on to go to Las Vegas. Meyer Lansky and his major associates never came anywhere near Newport. Day-to-day operations were in the hands of Ed Whitfield, Red Masterson, the Bermans, Louis Levinson and their employees.

CONCLUSION

In addition, despite the fact that casinos had large numbers of employees, the actual number of organized crime decision-makers was very small. Dealers at the Beverly Hills Club could not implicate Moe Dalitz in that operation. The farthest up the organized crime hierarchy any actual criminality could be traced might be to local managers. The local operators also ran small casinos, with few employees.

There are very practical reasons for this. First, small size and segmentation reduce the chances of getting caught and prosecuted. Since employees in illicit industries are the greatest threat to those operations and make the best witnesses against them, it is an organizational necessity for organized crime groups to limit the number of people who have knowledge about the group's operations. This is achieved, in part, by employing persons who only know about their own jobs and their own level of activity in the enterprise.

The history of organized crime in Newport also tells us that limited geographic reach also provides security for criminal enterprises. In Newport, casino operators were reluctant to even look across the river at their counterparts in Covington, less than a mile away in considering expansion. The Cleveland Four were the only inter-county syndicate, and that involved only one casino, the Lookout House, managed by a Kenton County local and regarded ultimately as an expendable property. It is true that Dalitz, Tucker Rothkopf, Kleinman, the Levinsons and the Bermans had other organized crime–related businesses in far-flung corners of the country. But those businesses involved different partners, different collaborators and different criminal syndicates than those that operated in Newport.

Limited geographic scope is vital because the larger the geographic area, the more tenuous communication becomes, requiring either the use of the telephone (and the threat of electronic surveillance) or long trips to pass on routine information in person, a most inefficient means of managing a business. This problem was manifest in Newport when syndicate leaders distanced themselves from local operations and those left in charge made very poor decisions, including the decision to frame Ratterman, the decision to distance themselves from the Committee of 500 and the decision to have Jack Theim raid the Playtorium. In addition, the larger the geographic area becomes, the greater the number of law enforcement agencies involved and the higher the costs of corruption. In Newport, corrupting one county and city government was easy, efficient and successful.

Organizational dynamics revolving around adaptability, flexibility, communications and timely responses also drive how organized crime structures itself. Despite popular media portrayals to the contrary, organized crime is made up of a series of highly adaptive, flexible networks that readily take into account changes in the law and regulatory practices, the growth or decline of market demand for a particular good or service and the availability of new sources of supply and new opportunities for distribution. Certainly this was true in Newport, where properties changed hands, individuals were assigned and reassigned and modes of operation were adapted to meet specific problem exigencies. The Cleveland Four's practice of closing casinos during grand jury meetings is a case in point, as is "Sleepout" Louis Levinson's decision to drop his liquor license in favor of a nonregulated milk bar.

Of course, organized crime also requires corruption and political influence. There is probably no city that demonstrates better than Newport the fact that organized criminals, legitimate businessmen and government officials are all equal players in a marketplace of corruption. The stability and longevity of corruption in Newport supports this market dynamic. In fact, it would be fair to argue, looking at the whole history of vice in Newport, that, far more than gambling and prostitution, corruption was the most valuable commodity produced and supplied.

Obviously, organized crime cannot be understood apart from the community in which operates. This is certainly true in Newport, where organized crime was in every way a community enterprise. Organized crime flourished in Newport because one, there was a market and two, there was a community need for productive, profit-making enterprises. In Newport, organized crime provided services that the legitimate world could not or would not supply. It supplied jobs for community residents. It provided supplemental income for persons on fixed low-income pensions or who had other economic problems. Casinos and handbooks required waitresses, clerks, technicians, bartenders and the like, not just in Newport's casinos and brothels, but in all the legitimate businesses that benefited from the presence of vice. Clearly, gamblers supported local businesses. In fact, at least from 1930 to 1960, gambling and prostitution profits allowed small shopkeepers to compete with chain stores and larger competitors.

Corruption, combined with strong leadership from organized crime networks, also serves as vital social control. It may be ironic, but organized crime groups provide an extremely effective means by which to control predator and violent crime. The small amount of violence over a three-decade span in Newport, a city full of criminal actors (the Beverly Hills fire, the Brady and Farley shootings and Screw Andrews's machinations) is testimony to the power of organized crime networks in keeping the community safe. In fact, cities in which corruption is maximized experience very rare and brief occurrences of organized crime–related violence.

CONCLUSION

Gambling, prostitution and other forms of vice didn't happen in Newport because "bad actors" forced them on the community. The casinos and the brothels provided very real economic and social benefits. It was only when those benefits began to wane that any type of reform became possible. Very successful criminals like Moe Dalitz and Meyer Lansky never operated where they were not wanted, and Newport wanted them very badly.

REFERENCES

Abadinsky, Howard. *Organized Crime*. 3rd ed. Chicago, IL: Nelson-Hall, 1994.

Albanese, Jay S. *Organized Crime in America*. 2nd ed. Cincinnati, OH: Anderson, 1989.

Albini, Joseph L. *The American Mafia: Genesis of a Legend*. New York: Appleton-Century-Crofts, 1971.

Anthony, Irvin. *Paddle Wheels and Pistols*. Philadelphia: Macrae Smith Co., 1929.

Asbury, Herbert. *The French Quarter: An Informal History of the New Orleans Underworld*. New York: Alfred A. Knopf, 1940.

———. *Sucker's Progress*. New York: Dodd, Mead and Company, Inc., 1938.

Associated Press. "Newport, Ky., Officials indicted on charges of permitting vice." *New York Times* September 14, 1961.

———. "Two are indicted in vice-raid case: Accused of conspiracy to cause Ratterman's arrest." *New York Times*, May 27, 1961.

———. "Wide open town faces shut-down: Many Newport, Ky. Officials indicted in clean-up." *New York Times*, September 24, 1961.

Atkinson, Geo W. *After the Moonshiners: By One of the Raiders*. Wheeling, WV: Steam Book and Job Printers, 1881.

Bancroft, Frederic. *Slave Trading in the Old South*. Baltimore, MD: J.H. Furst, 1931.

Barker, Thomas, and Marjie Britz. *Jokers Wild: Legalized Gambling the Twenty-First Century*. New York: Praeger, 2000.

REFERENCES

Barnes, Margaret Anne. *The Tragedy and the Triumph of Phenix City, Alabama.* Macon, GA: Mercer University Press, 1998.

Behr, E.J. *Prohibition: Thirteen Years That Changed America.* New York: Arcade Publishing, 1996.

Benedict, J. 2000. http://www.netmar.com/~creator/benedict/.

Bingham, W. "Gambling unchecked in North Kentucky: Expert claims use of marked cards, crooked dice to Senate investigators." *Louisville Courier Journal,* August 22, 1961.

———. "3 Kentucky witnesses use the 5th 79 times: 2 threatened with contempt of Congress as Senate group studies state gambling." *Louisville Courier Journal,* August 30, 1961.

———. "11 Newport (Ky.) Officials acquitted of conspiracy." *New York Times,* December 18, 1963.

———. "Ratterman new Kentucky sheriff." *New York Times,* November 8, 1961.

———. "Reform ticket captures posts in Kentucky county." *New York Times,* November 6, 1963.

———. "Two are convicted in civil rights plot." *New York Times,* August 7, 1963.

Blackman, C. "Speaker focuses on pirate James Ford's links to Crenshaw." *Harrisburg Daily Register,* August 8, 1997.

Block, Alan A. *East Side-West Side: Organizing Crime in New York, 1930–1950.* New Brunswick, NJ: Transaction, 1978.

Block, Alan A., and William J. Chambliss. *Organizing Crime.* New York: Elsevier, 1981.

Carr, Jess. *The Second Oldest Profession: An Informal History of Moonshining in America.* Englewood Cliffs, NJ: Prentice-Hall, 1972.

Chalfant, Frank E. "Treasures of Nostalgia." 2000. http://home.swbell.net/treanost/index.html.

Chambliss, William J. *On The Take: From Petty Crooks to Presidents.* 2nd ed. Bloomington, IN: Indiana University Press, 1988.

Cincinnati Post. 1999. "Ex-Newport Bluesman Charles Brown Dies." January 26.

Clark, Thomas D. *Agrarian Kentucky.* Lexington: University Press of Kentucky, 1977.

———. *Kentucky: Land of Contrast.* New York: Harper and Row, 1968.

"Close Encounters: An Interview with Frank Benton." 2003. http://www.insidenorthernkentucky.com/yourTown/YourTown1002/CloseEncounters.htm.

REFERENCES

Coates, Robert M. *The Outlaw Years: The History of the Land Pirates of the Natchez Trace.* New York: The Literary Guild of America, 1930.

Coleman, J. Winston. "Lexington's slave dealers and their Southern trade." *Filson Club History Quarterly* 12, (January 1938): 9–10.

———. *Slavery Times in Kentucky.* Chapel Hill: University of North Carolina Press, 1954.

Combs, B. Executive Order (61-815). October 10, 1961.

———. Executive Order (61-816). October 10, 1961.

Committee of 500. Letter to George Ratterman. October 11, 1961.

Cullen, K. "Newport unsure of nude-dancing ban's effect." *Cincinnati Enquirer*, March 20, 1983.

Dabney, Joseph Earl. *Mountain Spirits: A Chronicle of Corn Whiskey from King James' Ulster Plantation to America's Appalachins and the Moonshine Life.* New York: Charles Scribner's Sons, 1974.

Davidson, B. "The Great Kentucky Scandal." *Saturday Evening Post*, October 21, 1961.

DeVol, George H. *Forty Years a Gambler on the Mississippi.* New York: H. Holt & Company.

DeVroomen, S. "Newport approves public nudity ban." *Kentucky Post*, July 16, 1991.

Donovan, Frank Robert. *River Boats of America.* New York: Thomas Y. Crowell Company, 1966.

Eckert, Allan W. *Dark and Bloody River: Chronicles of the Ohio River Valley.* New York: Bantam, Doubleday, Dell, 1996.

Episal, J. 2000. http://www.unshreddednostalgia.com/.

Farmer, E. and P. Welch. "Evelyn reveals Clark killing story." *Cincinnati Post*, September 28, 1955.

Fried, Albert. *The Rise and Fall of the Jewish Gangster in America.* New York: Holt, Rinehart and Winston, 1980.

Fry, M. "Cross Section U.S.A.: Sin Town–Complacent Newport, Kentucky." *Esquire* XLVII, 8 (May 1957).

Giordano, R. "Report from Monmouth Street." *Enquirer*, September 7, 1980.

Goldfarb, Ronald L. *Perfect Villains, Imperfect Heroes: Robert Kennedy's War Against Organized Crime.* New York: Random House, 1995.

Grady, Alan. *When Good Men Do Nothing: The Assassination of Albert Patterson.* Tuscaloosa: University of Alabama Press, 2003.

Griffith, George P. *Life and Adventures of Revenooer No. 1.* Birmingham, AL: Gander Publishers, 1975.

Hall, E. "Anna's War Against River Pirates and Cave Bandits of John A. Murrell's Northern Drive." Unpublished manuscript, Southern Illinois University, Rare Book Collections, n.d.

Haller, M. "Illegal Enterprise: A Theoretical and Historical Interpretation." *Criminology* 28, 2 (1990): 207–35.

Harrisburg Daily Register. 1997. "Hold the salt: Crenshaw's 200th birthday, actions recalled." November 19.

Havighurst, Walter. *Voices on the River, The Story of Mississippi Waterways.* New York: Macmillan Company, 1964.

Hertel. Ed. "Ed Hertel's Guide to Illegal Gaming Clubs and Chips." http://www.chipster.net/index.htm.

Hinton, H. "Kentucky official says he's a bookie." *New York Times,* July 24, 1951.

————. "Senators warn Florida governor to talk on crime or face action." *New York Times,* June 21, 1951.

Hodges, Juanita. Written Affidavit by Juanita Hodges, n.d.

Horstman, B.M. "George Ratterman: He's the man who cleaned up Newport." *Cincinnati Post*, August 12, 1999.

Hunter, J. "All Organized Crime Isn't the Mafia: A Case Study of a Non-Traditional Criminal Organization." Paper given at the Academy of Criminal Justice Sciences, San Antonio, Texas, March 1983.

Insight. 1987. "Rehabilitating a Reputation: A Born-again City on the Ohio." January 12.

Kellner, Esther. *Moonshine: Its History and Folklore.* Indianapolis, IN: Bobbs-Merrill Co., 1971.

Kentucky Post. 1931. "Cammack leads raids on three Abig shot@ dens: Attorney General leads officers into dives crowded with gamblers; Fuller silent on action of state and criticism of officials." June 30.

————. 1981. "Newport's bright lights are going dim. 1981." October 1981.

Kentucky State Police. "Raid on the Lookout House." Supplementary Report, case number H-420-3, 1952.

Kobler, J. "King of the moonshiners." *Saturday Evening Post*, August 2, 1958.

Laudeman, Jeff. "Diceman.net." http://www.diceman.net/.

————. *The Real Sin City.* JSL Publishing, 1997.

Lazarus, T. http://www.ocvirtual.com/cotob.

Long, P.A. "Court helps douse heat in 'Sin City.'" *Cincinnati Post*, June 24, 1991.

Louisville Courier-Journal. 1962. "Former mayor and others fined total of $59.250 in Newport gambling case: Many get jail sentences of six months, probated; Conspiracy trial Sept. 10. 1962." August 22.

Marshall, Theodora Britton, and Gladys Crail Evans. *They Found It in Natchez.* New Orleans: Pelican Publishing Company, 1939.

Mastrofski, S., and G. Potter. "Controlling organized crime: A critique of public policy. *Policy Studies Review* 2, 3 (1987): 269–301.

Maurer, David W. *Kentucky Moonshine.* Lexington: Kentucky University Press, 1974.

Maxwell, J. "Newport: Sin city, revisited." *Kentucky Enquirer*, 1960. Reprinted from the *Saturday Evening Post.*

McGee, J. "A Cavern of Crime." *Livingston Ledger*, 1973.

Messick, Hank. "Big casinos continue to operate on guarded basis at Newport: Having no licenses to revoke they're not worried about ABC." *Louisville Courier-Journal*, April 12, 1961.

———. "Campbell jury indicts sheriff and 4 others: Charges officials aware of widespread gambling but failed to suppress it." *Louisville Courier-Journal*, November 16, 1961.

———. "Car bombed at antivice residence: Newport abuzz after woman seriously hurt." *Louisville Courier-Journal*, April 29, 1961.

———. "500 felony charges will be prepared for Campbell jury: 45 misdemeanor counts returned by panel before adjourning until August 31." *Louisville Courier-Journal*, August 22, 1961.

———. "Former marshal names Mr. Big of Newport: Syndicate in control, Harris tells reporters; Grand jury hears Wise." *Louisville Courier-Journal*, September 12, 1961.

———. "IRS agents arrest 4 here, 2 in Covington in gambling raids: Drive staged over nation." *Louisville Courier-Journal*, June 29, 1961.

———. "Judge acquits Carcini, Paisley: Says no evidence presented in Ratterman conspiracy case." *Louisville Courier-Journal*, June 20, 1961.

———. Letter to Mr. Pope, n.d.

———. *The Mobs and the Mafia.* New York: Ballantine, 1972.

———. "Police hunt witnesses at Newport: Combs orders state troopers to make search." *Louisville Courier-Journal*, August 30, 1961.

———. *The Private Lives of Public Enemies.* New York: P.H. Wyden, 1973.

———. *Razzle Dazzle.* Covington: For the Love of Books, 1995.

———. "Robert Kennedy says Newport gambling big." *Louisville Courier-Journal*, June 25, 1961.

———. "Self-portrait: Kindly syndicate wants to chase the bad guys out of Newport." *Louisville Courier-Journal*, June 15, 1961.

REFERENCES

———. "Sensational testimony expected from Wilder ex-marshal today: He'll appear at Newport." *Louisville Courier Journal*, September 7, 1961.

———. *The Silent Syndicate*. New York: Macmillan, 1967.

———. *Syndicate Wife*. New York: Tower, 1968.

Miller, Wilbur R. *Revenuers & Moonshiners: Enforcing Federal Liquor Law in the Mountain South, 1865–1900*. Chapel Hill: University of North Carolina Press, 1991.

Montell, William Lynwood. *The Saga of Coe Ridge: A Study in Oral History*. Knoxville: University of Tennessee Press, 1970.

Morris. H. "Four swank Newport clubs turn to dry gambling: Operate without drink permits; State can't act." *Louisville Courier Journal*, April 16, 1961.

Neumeister, L. "Mayor hopes to clean up Newport's night life." *Cincinnati Enquirer*, July 11, 1982.

Newport Police Department. "Arrest report from April Flowers, George Ratterman, and Tito Carcini." May 9, 1961.

New York Times. 1951. "Police chief hunted: Kentucky official face call in Senate crime inquiry." July 22.

———. 1951. "Two gamblers balk at senate questions." June 20.

Pearce, John Ed. *Divide and Dissent: Kentucky Politics 1930–1963*. Lexington: University Press of Kentucky, 1987.

Potter, Gary W. *Criminal Organizations*. Prospects Heights, IL: Waveland Press, 1994.

Potter, Gary W., and Philip Jenkins. *The City and the Syndicate: Organizing Crime in Philadelphia*. Lexington, MA: Ginn Press, 1985.

———. "The politics and mythology of organized crime: A Philadelphia case study." *Journal of Criminal Justice* 15, 4 (1987).

Potter, Gary W., and T. Cox. "A community paradigm of organized crime." *American Journal of Criminal Justice* XV, 1 (1990): 1–23.

Prendergast, J. "Big N. Ky. trafficker arrested, police say." *Cincinnati Enquirer*, March 3, 1999.

Purvis, T.L., ed. With coauthors K.M. Clift, B.M. Daniels, E.P. Fennel and M.E. Whitehead. *Newport, Kentucky: A Bicentennial History*. Newport, KY.: Otto Zimmerman & Sons, 1996.

Rankin, Hugh F. *The Golden Age of Piracy*. New York: Holt, Rinehart & Winston, 1969.

Reis, J. "Turmoil, tragedy defined congressional race of '66." *Kentucky Post*, May 30, 2003.

Reuter, Peter. *Disorganized Crime*. Cambridge, MA: MIT Press, 1983.

REFERENCES

Rochester Daily Advertiser. 1830. "Boat-Wreckers or Banditti of the West." January 29.

Roe, C. *Panderers and Their White Slaves*. Chicago: Revell Publishing Company, 1922.

Rothert, Otto Arthur. *The Outlaws of Cave-in-Rock*. Cleveland, OH: Arthur H. Clark Co., 1924.

Schmidt, W. "New era, New problems for south's sheriffs." *New York Times*, September 10, 1984.

Schroeder, C. "Newport adult club shut down: Prostitution alleged at Trixie's." *Cincinnati Enquirer*, 1988.

———. "Newport seeks to regulate massage parlors." *Cincinnati Enquirer*, February 4, 1988.

Sherry, Frank. *Raiders and Rebels*. New York: Hearst Marine Books, 1986.

"Sin City." *Esquire Magazine* (May 1957).

Smith, Dwight C. *The Mafia Mystique*. New York: Basic Books, 1974.

Snively, William Daniel. *Satan's Ferryman: A True Tale of the Old Frontier*. New York, NY: Frederick Ungar, 1968.

St. George, D. "Miss. trial renews tale of Southern underworld." *Louisville Courier-Journal*, October 14, 1991.

Tabor, P. *Pauline's*. Lousville, KY: Touchstone, 1971.

Thompson, Buddy. *Madam Belle Brezing*. Lexington, KY: Buggy Whip Press, 1983.

United Press International. "FBI seizes 3,457 slots, arrests 32 persons in raids in score of Kentucky cities: Devices worth a million are picked up." *New York Times*, January 19, 1952.

———. "5 Newport, Ky.. Officials acquitted at bribery trial." *New York Times*, November 14, 1963.

———. "Kentucky troopers called out in emergency action on rackets." *New York Times*, August 31, 1961.

———. "Mayor and council indicted in Newport, Ky, scandal." *New York Times*, November 1, 1963.

———. "Six in Newport, Ky. Charged in plot for false arrest." *New York Times*, October 28, 1961.

———. "Two acquitted in plot to frame candidate." *New York Times*, June 21, 1961.

United States District Court (Eastern District of Kentucky). *Report of the Grand Jury*. March Term (Covington), 1953.

Weems, C. *A Breed Apart*. Tabor City, NC: Atlantic Printing, 1992.

Winick, Charles, and Paul M. Kinise. *The Lively Commerce: Prostitution in the United States*. Chicago: Quadrangle Books, 1971.

Cases

Commonwealth v. Murphy. 295 Ky. 466; 174 S.W. (K.Y. 1943).

Commonwealth v. Wise. 351 S. W. 2d 493 (K. Y. 1961).

Lester v. Kentucky Bar Association. 32 S.W. 2d 435 (K.Y. 1975).

Ratterman v. Stapleton. 371 S.W. 2d 939 (K.Y. 1963).

Sidell et al., Appellants v. Hill, Appellee. 357 S. W. 2d 318 (K.Y. 1962).

U.S. v. Andrews, Owens, Andrews, Whitley, Postell, Tye, Andriola, Malone. 347 F. 2d.

True Tales of Old-Time Kentucky Politics

Bombast, Bourbon and Burgoo

By Berry Craig • ISBN 978-1-59629-636-7 • 6 x 9" • 128 pages
Over 40 images • $19.99

Discover fascinating and little-known stories from Kentucky's political past.

Join longtime columnist Berry Craig as he shares tales of a time when votes could be bought with a drink and political differences were resolved with ten paces and a pistol.

Visit us at
www.historypress.net